Your Words are Powerful
Be Careful What You Speak

I AM JUST A VESSEL:
ENCOURAGEMENT FOR 365 DAYS

Suzi Yelvington

TRILOGY CHRISTIAN PUBLISHERS

TUSTIN, CA

Trilogy Christian Publishers
A Wholly Owned Subsidary of Trinity Broadcasting Network
2442 Michelle Drive
Tustin, CA 92780

Your Words are Powerful, Be Careful What You Speak

Rights Department, 2442 Michelle Drive, Tustin, CA 92780.

Trilogy Christian Publishing/TBN and colophon are trademarks of Trinity Broadcasting Network.

For information about special discounts for bulk purchases, please contact Trilogy Christian Publishing.

Trilogy Disclaimer: The views and content expressed in this book are those of the author and may not necessarily reflect the views and doctrine of Trilogy Christian Publishing or the Trinity Broadcasting Network. Contents and/or cover may not be reproduced in whole or in part in any form without express written consent.

Manufactured in the United States of America

10 9 8 7 6 5 4 3 2 1

Library of Congress Cataloging-in-Publication Data is available.

ISBN: 979-8-89041-342-0

E-ISBN: 979-8-89041-343-7

Acknowledgments

I would like to acknowledge and thank

Jenny Van Auken, Creative Director
Trish Herndon, Graphics
MaryJo Kelley, editor

for their assistance and insight while working on this book.

Each of you should use whatever gift you have received to serve others, as faithful stewards of God's grace in its various forms.

1 Peter 4:10 (NIV)

A vessel of the Lord is one who receives graces.
Angels interact with us through God's vessels.
We can all be called upon to serve as a vessel of the Lord by speaking God's Word.
This one-year devotional is Suzi's daily prayer journal.
Each morning God directs her pen as she reads His Word.
This gift He has bestowed upon her serves as a motivation to others to walk in faith.
Trust in the Lord, as He has created each of us intentionally.
As a steward of the gift you have received from God, use it to serve one another.

Praise for *Words are Powerful, Be Careful What You Speak* from devoted Facebook Followers:

Somehow, these daily readings are spot on... like Suzi is in my head, processing my thoughts and struggles from the day before and hugging my heart for what the day might bring. Her inspirational words are just what I need to reflect, recharge and rejoice. I love that she is "real." Because we are real, all of us...fighting hard battles, putting on a smile sometimes when we really want to cry.

Thank you, Suzi, for helping me start each day off right.

—Kelly C.

Read [Suzi's] writings, be encouraged, and follow [her] daily for beautiful, real, relevant, and timeless recommendations directly out of her personal journey.

—Donna D.

These writings are not just words. When [Suzi] write[s], it brings restoration ... people read, understand, and the Holy Spirit brings revelation.

—Jacqueline P.

Prayers are truly the best for seeking peace and comfort; thank you once again for starting my day off with promise.

—Candace D.

Your messages are awesome. So fresh, poignant, and honest! I am so grateful I [have these messages] every morning to kick it in gear and motivate [me]...

—Donna

He will cause the "overflow" of your ministry to heal, restore and make alive those around you...All because "you were just a vessel."

—Jodi B. G.

Contents

A Note to the Reader

From humble beginnings, I learned through observation the type of woman I wanted to become and transformed instead of conformed to the mighty woman of God I am today. My strong belief in empowering people, especially women, comes from a place of growth through experience: self-discipline, dedication, and determination. I seek guidance from the Holy Spirit for all that I do. I am a firm believer in, "But seek first the kingdom of God and His righteousness, and all these things shall be added to you" (Matthew 6:33, NKJV). By beginning each morning with prayer and contemplation, I established a lifelong routine of inviting the Holy Spirit under my roof. The Lord called me to begin this ministry with texts to my children each morning. My children, in turn, began sharing my daily message with others. As more began requesting the Word, I sent my messages via text messaging and social media to reach a continually grow-ing community. I am blessed to send my own "download from heaven" to my followers each day.

My messages now travel around the world, passed from my social media followers to their friends and family. For almost a decade, I have been invited into the homes and lives of many. By request, I compiled many of my messages into a yearlong devotional book. It is my desire for the Holy Spirit to transform lives through the renewal of one's mind and refreshing of their spirit. My work is entirely the power of the Holy Spirit. I cannot take any credit. God gets all the glory. We are all a part of social networking that can give hope, encouragement, and love. This is how we can show support for one another. I appreciate your support, and I want to thank you for following me and allowing me to share my story of faith. I cannot express how grateful I feel. I give God all the glory from the bottom of my heart. There are no simple solutions to life's problems. It is a fight of faith that gives you hope and trust in the only One who holds your future in His hands. We are in this Life together! Iron sharpens iron.

January

So, shall My word be that goes forth out of My mouth: It shall not return to Me void, but it shall accomplish that which I please and purpose, and it shall prosper in the thing for which I sent it.

Isaiah 55:11 (NKJV; paraphrased)

Your words are powerful. Be careful what you speak.

JANUARY 1

It is time to rise! The way you see God shows up just in the way you live your life. You cannot outgrow scripture. It deepens and widens with age. Broken to God means beautiful. Saturate yourself with the Word, and you will look out for others and not be saturated with only yourself. Carry your own cross and grow. Be as quick to start your day with a kneel as you are to text! The ideal Christian is not to be happy but to be Holy Spirit-filled. Ask yourself, what do I want to be doing when Christ comes back? You should never need to hide anything in your life if you are right with God. If you have stopped repenting, then you have stopped growing. Real peace is willing to obey His voice. Compromising will make you look like the man in the world. I have been driven to my knees with overwhelming tests, only to find out that was where I found my help!

I declare: "I will kneel before God and obey His voice in my silence."

JANUARY 2

Calling things luck cheapens all the wonderworking supernatural power that God has just freely given to you as a part of His miraculous plan. *Dream!* There is no cheat code to anything that is worth anything in your precious life! It will take lots of hard work, discipline, and commitment to refine your flesh to get spiritually connected to our loving God. Your personal breakthrough that you have been waiting for will begin this new season of a change in your belief system. Right now, make an effort to turn that one weakness into a strength. Today is not that day to stop trying. That test will make you a much better person. Keep yourself clean and bright. The easy way out does not ever work. It will only make things more difficult in the long run. Perseverance will be your engine, and it will propel your hope. This problem is a test to do your best. Rise, rise, rise! Be that champion and move forward! We cannot become what we need to be for the work of God by remaining what we are! Life always offers you a second chance... it is called today! When faithful in teeny tiny little things, God will make you ruler over much and equipped with Holy Spirit's power.

I declare: "I will press through whatever I need to do today."

JANUARY 3

Unplug and shut off your phone, say a prayer, and say it aloud so you can finally be alone with God. Declare: "Take control of what I say, O Lord, and guard my lips today. Lord, empty me of me so I can be filled with You." When God calls you to grow, He will make you uncomfortable. Follow the conviction of the Holy Spirit. Listen; the voice of God will never contradict with the Word of God. The new year will be all about bettering myself and my relationship with God! I am ready and temporarily closed for Holy Spiritual Maintenance. Be ready for above the ordinary, mighty for God. Ask God for a dream. Ask God for wisdom. All surpassing power is from God and not from us. Be still! Just trust God.

I declare: "I will be thoughtful of every word I speak or I am about to speak."

JANUARY 4

You are called with a "Holy Calling." Seek His will in everything you do! Everything. Stay at peace with all your neighbors. Some people may not change, but that has nothing to do with you. Love is what you do, not what you say. It is never wrong to do the right thing. A relationship with no trust is a cell phone with no service. Morals, intelligence, and class cannot be bought with money. How you are to others when you are in a beautiful positive position of success will dictate how God will be to you. Stay gracious, kind, forgiving, and loving even when you are betrayed. God will provide for you! Love and forgive! He has set before us a blessing or a cursing; God says to choose *life!* No matter what!

I declare: "I will show love in "all" situations; it's empowering!"

JANUARY 5

Some things you can only learn in a storm. What makes you come alive? The world needs people who have come alive with their dream. Build someone up today. Life is right now. Your enthusiasm about life is the root of all beautiful things. Avoid complaining, gossiping, envying, comparing, doubting, fearing, and hating. All relationships are never wasted. They bring you what you need or teach you what you do not need. People will never forget how you make them feel. Surround yourself with the inspired, the gracious, the grateful, and the ones who serve others. Be much stronger than your excuses. Unlock others' potential. Not all storms disrupt; some have come to clear the way to your new destiny. Be aware. Declare: I am ready to grow and get better. I am physically, mentally, and emotionally ready to enter a new phase in my life. Write your thoughts down. God has given you the Holy Spirit to be able to do all of this!

I declare: "I will go out of my way to make someone feel fabulous, tell a stranger how beautiful they are, etc...."

It's amazing how beautiful you will feel.

JANUARY 6

I think Sunday is the most important day of the week. A relationship with the Lord is the most important relationship you can have. Embrace it every day, not just on Sunday. Church is a hospital for broken hearts and people. If a church hurt your heart and it has caused you to lose your faith in the Lord, well, then maybe your faith was in church, people, and not in Jesus. Do not stop worshiping God on Sunday at church because of others' behavior. God is always the same! It is people that change. Sin will fascinate before it assassinates. Let God put you back together right in front of the ones that broke you. You are somebody's blessing. A Sunday routine will change your life. Do not start your week feeling unprepared. It is okay to do some prepping, planning, or catching up on Sunday. To avoid the Monday full blues, do not let a Sunday go without worshiping our God in a corporate setting. It is so important to set aside time for God. Wherever worshiping is for you, do it every Sunday and preferably a little every day. If you are like me, always wanting to improve and making the most of every day.

I declare: "I will set aside time daily for God, but Sunday, I will corporately (go to church) worship Him."

JANUARY 7

Today is a blank page! Make it a good one. Whatever you decide to do, work it with all your heart, as working for the Lord, not for human masters. My God will supply all of my needs. Declare: I am surrounded by God's favor. And we do know that in all things, God works for the good of those who love Him. For God will be pleased with me when I do what I know is right. Right now, this very moment, my God is lining things up for me. He always has, and, I believe, He always will. The Holy Spirit will lead me. God does not want you to try harder. He wants you to trust Him deeper through it all. Stop trying so hard. Do start trusting and just believing. This, right here, will change everything right now in you. To write from the heart of the Holy Spirit you have, to endure and embrace the creative power from the comforter, and to position whatever He shows you. So, when all else fails, write what He tells you. You cannot depend on your eyes. You must pray and wait for a fresh new vision and then look again to believe He has filled your basket and given you a fresh new birthing for what you believe you will live this year, starting right now in Him! All the glory and praise go to our God!

I declare: "I am blessed and 'highly' favored; favor tracks me down in 'all' areas of my life."

JANUARY 8

It is your responsibility for the length of time to let what has hurt you haunt you. Best friends communicate and really talk about things, whether good or bad. They appreciate the flaws and love you unconditionally. If you act the same way they did, then how will others tell the difference between you and them? I am convinced that nothing can ever separate us from God's love. Think of how wonderfully you have grown since January of last year. Faith is not an emotion. It is a firm decision made by me to stand on the Word of God no matter what I hear or see. If they have wronged you, they need your prayers so much more, and if they are enemies, then you are ordered by God to release them and pray for them. In this fear-filled earth, we strongly need to be the fearless church. God wants our hearts to be childlike and our heads to act grown up! Every nanosecond, we should be totally dependent on our mighty God!

I declare: "I will operate out of love and rise above all situations."

JANUARY 9

Declare: I am a doer. I am a thinker. I see possibilities. You have value. You are potential. You are amazing. Believe. Your current circumstances are a part of the divine plan God has for you. You have not because you have asked not. Commit all you do unto the Lord, and your thoughts shall be established to do so. If I waited for perfection, I would never write. I am always writing something in my head. I fail only if I decide to stop writing. And sometimes only paper listens. I write daily to make it a habit. And when I sit down to write, I know I am doing the thing I was created to do. When it is real, you cannot walk away from it. Pray over your God-given dream. Life goes by fast, not to do what you are called to do. Blessed is the one who reads aloud the Word of God. Blessed are the ones who hear it and do it. Do not water the weeds in your life. Live like you love yourself. Never repeat regrets. Avoid loose talk. Wise people do not make a show of their knowledge. Work hard and become a leader. Use helpful words and stay away from anything harmful. The more you invite the Holy Spirit in your life, the happier and the healthier you will become. Pleasant words are sweet to your soul and healing to your bones.

I declare: "I am a doer, I am a thinker, I have potential, and I am valued."

JANUARY 10

Wait until all the pieces of the puzzle come together, and then you will understand what you have been through. It will happen all of a sudden! I have a feeling you are about to be happier than you have ever been. Watch God's next move. God is nudging you to release that crazy worry, that negative stress. You will meet that right person at the right time to help you grow. Those closed doors will open again. Depart from evil and press into God's wisdom. That private struggle will be a public testimony of God's supernatural, preternatural, paranormal power to turn these things around. Slam the door on things that do not help you. God will restore, but first, we have to be obedient. God can break the bad cycles. I declare your personal situation will make a turn for the very best. With God, *all things* are possible to those who put their total trust in Him and believe. I know God has amazing plans; pray for direction to follow them. Your career will prosper. Your body will be healed. No weapon formed against you shall prosper, in Jesus' name. Touch the hem of God's garment! Just stand still and believe. The Word of God is life! It's powerful! Dare to trust Him.

I declare: "I am declaring a sudden of supernatural wisdom and guidance to move me forward."

JANUARY 11

Stop being the general manager of life! If anything is happening that is amazing, we should marvel and praise God! It is He who does the miracles. He makes all the moves. He is the Creator of the universe. "How great You are, oh Lord!" I love it because this is the day that the Lord has made, and it is our responsibility to rejoice and be happy. He will supply us with His benefits daily by trusting Him to do so. Two things will prevent you from happiness, staying stuck in the past and comparing yourself to others. It is the bad things that inspire you to change and grow. Perseverance is failing forty-nine times and succeeding the fiftieth. Trying is risking failure. If you do not try, you ensure failure. Finally, dwell on whatever is true, noble, right, pure, lovely, admirable, excellent, and praiseworthy. Think about these things. Dwell on them! Tell the truth to yourself. Live as the warrior.

I declare: "I will trust the Lord with 'everything' in my life."

JANUARY 12

Give yourself some credit for how far you have come today. A few nice words can really launch you into a new season.

Whatever you do, do not sit still. Constantly *grow*! Find you're equal! That is what makes you whole! Love your whole entire life. The gold was that day you said, "I am really going to do this." Choose to see the beauty in it all! That is how everything is connected. *Forgiveness* is *freedom*. Forgive them. Forgive her. Forgive him. Now you just took back your power. Be easy on others, just like you are easy on yourself. Alone or not, you have got to move forward. Let's go. Give thanks in all circumstances; for this is the will of God in Christ Jesus for you.

I declare: "I will seek the Holy Spirit and ask Him to reveal to me who I need to forgive. I am living in freedom by forgiving those."

JANUARY 13

Be very careful about what you are thinking. Those thoughts are running your life, and if they are negative, they are ruining your life. Your beauty should be your inner self, with gentleness, and a quiet spirit, which is of great worth in God's sight. So be careful how you live. Do not live like a fool. Do not act thoughtlessly. Stay in understanding of what the Lord will have you do. Do not be disappointed, for God is right with you. To everything, there is a season and a time to every purpose. The Lord looks down upon a proud look, a lying tongue, hands that go against the innocent, and a heart that devises wicked plans. The fear of the Lord is the beginning of the greatest wisdom ever. Being cheerful keeps you healthy. It is a slow death to be gloomy all the time. Make it your goal to live a quiet life, minding your own business and working with your own hands, just as you were instructed to do so. Refresh others.

I declare: "I will take every thought captive and not dwell on anything negative."

JANUARY 14

You cannot stay trapped in your old destructive ways.

First part of the day—give it all to God! And my favorite verse for years has been, "Seek the Kingdom of God above *all* else, and He will give you everything you need" (Matthew 6:33, NKJV; paraphrased). There is power in His name! And now, several years later, this verse will be my forever favorite one. I give God complete control over my whole life, myself, my marriage, my family, and my day. I remain humble and in prayer this way. Never stop praying. There is no better way to live; trust His Word! He gives me everything I need, not everything I want to have! Keep seeking Him over your whole life and goals. He is the way, the truth, the life. In our house, hard work matters. The difference between need and want is self-control and you seeking God first. This is the joy of spiritual growth.

I declare: "I am moving forward this year!"

JANUARY 15

Celebrate when you see others doing well, and do not speak when they do wrong. Encourage them! Avoid that idle talk, and you will stay out of trouble! Zipper! Have you heard a rumor? Let it lay low, be smart; it will be okay not to speak it. It is a great thing to just mind your own business. People who hurt others only hurt themselves in the long run. That is why minding your own business is so amazing. Wait patiently for the Lord to help you! He can lift you out of the pit. Life will disappoint you. Nothing can keep you unhappy if you do not want to be unhappy. It is a choice to change. One loyal friend is like good medicine. Once rested, get up and get busy. I pray that God, the source of *all happiness*, will completely fill you with abundant joy, peace, and hope. You are now overflowing with confidence and hope through the power of the Holy Spirit! Live by the Word of God, and you will produce amazing fruit in your life. We will never outgive God!

I declare: "I will put the zipper on and only speak encouragement. I will mind my own business."

JANUARY 16

Do not deliberately torture yourself by giving into that spirit of depression. Happiness makes for a long life and makes it worth living. Enjoy today! It is a gift! Worry does no good at all, and it has destroyed many people. It also will make you old before your time. Anger and jealousy will also shorten your life. Stay cheerful with that amazing attitude so you can have a good appetite and enjoy your food. This is key to staying happy and healthy. Entrust yourself and everyone else to God. You cannot do anything anyway; you are exactly where you need to be! The Lord hears His people when they call! I depend on God alone. He is my defender, and I will not be defeated. Be very careful about what you think. Do not use your mouth for destroying yourself.

I declare: "I will not worry or think about tomorrow."

JANUARY 17

Your limit is you. Time is not waiting for you. Declare: I am going to be myself 100 percent in all I do today. I am joy-filled. I am confident. I believe this year is full of things for you and me that have never been. Lose the fear. Use the negativity as positivity to fuel you to make those changes for the good. I honestly do not wake up every morning ready to go. I wake up and tell myself to mind my own business and take authority over my thoughts and words immediately. It is called the battle in your mind. The more I expand my positive mindset, the more self-controlled I am. To be a successful warrior, you take your average man and encourage him to be laser-like focused on the Word of God. Shift yourself to who you were created to be. Each time you feel disappointed, you lost the very best moment of a lifetime. You cannot major in minors. Stop wasting time. You have a powerful driving force inside of you that you can unleash your God-given dream with; it is called the Holy Spirit. Stop every thought that is not pushing your mind set in the God-given direction. "No" simply means begin again at working out of your higher nature. Do not quit! This next chapter is going to be an amazing purpose. Accept no one's definition of you. Look in God's Word.

I declare: "I will let go of what anyone has ever said about who I am. I believe I am who the Lord says I am."

JANUARY 18

Those ordinary hardships you are facing right now are making you extraordinary for a purpose of destiny. Excuses are knocking at your door. Excuses will always be lurking around to attach themselves to you. Be wise. Opportunity will not last. Complain...remain. Find a way to move ahead. If not, that excuse will blind you. I have made several mistakes in my life, but I did not ever quit. You just must make it happen. And you can start over this new day! Lack of communication with God can ruin a lot of great things. First on my daily list is to talk to God. He has always been my Rock. I like me better when I am with Jesus. I must leave everything in His hands. We are not called to live or be like others. We are called to be like Him. He loved me at my darkest. God can heal a broken heart, spirit, and body, but He must have all the pieces. I accept myself unconditionally. Fall in love with taking care of you. I believe.

I declare: "No excuses. I will do what I need to do to accomplish my goals."

JANUARY 19

When asked about your first love, I pray you say your own name. That would be the most beautiful thing above everything else. Sadly enough, most lose themselves in trying to people please others. One of my goals is to love myself and who I was created to be. Stop feeling invisible. To you, who has lost your faith in God. To you, who does not think you can hold on one more minute. This is just for you! You are amazing. You make the world you live in a more beautiful place. You have so many God-given gifts. You have so much more to do. You have wonderful time left. The best is yet to come, so here is what you need to do! Take a deep breath and hang in there. I believe you can do it. Declare: I can do all things through Christ who strengthens me. It is a matter of time when you will feel happy again. I pray that you will look in the mirror and remind yourself how incredible you really are. You are not damaged; you are wiser for what you have been through. There is strength in your scars. You have learned to leave people better than you found them, and that is your strength. The most attractive thing about you is how you make others feel when you leave. I am attracted to laughter. You are in the process of becoming more of who God made you to be. Masterpiece, that is me. You are not boring!

I declare: "I am worthy, I love myself for who I am and who I am becoming."

JANUARY 20

Intimidation is a spirit, and it is not from God. When it attacks, you may start to feel ashamed or worthless, but you must move on in your faith in God. The Word says several times, "*Fear not.*" God gives us power, love, and a sound mind. Guard your heart and mind towards the Lord and what He says about you. Stop being a coward and letting fear and intimidation rule you. Encourage yourself daily in the Lord. Build up your faith, and remember, only you can do this for yourself. Only you can stir your gift up. If someone does not love your spirit, bless them, and move on. Not everyone deserves your presence. Finish your race on earth, having kept the faith. You are a vessel. Stay set apart.

I declare: "I will be a peacemaker everywhere I go."

JANUARY 21

Enjoy family time. We charge our phones daily while our relationships die. Cell phones connect us to distant ones as they steal us from the one we are with. Talk about the future God has for you. Until someone unlocks their cell phone for you, do not unlock the four chambers of your beautiful heart. Today, you can touch each other, but not each other's phones. Your cell has already replaced your: calendar, computer, alarm clock, banking, and calculator; please do not let it replace family or sweet relationships. Relationships suffer when texting replaces talking. Break up with your cell phone and become engaged with the folks you are with. Never make the one you are with feel alone, especially when you are right there with them. I love hanging out with people that make me forget to look at my phone. Give loved ones your life, as a gift of your presence, by putting down your mobile device. Life happens when you put your phone down. Intercession is one of the most important ways we can release the power of God into the lives of others by talking and praying for them. Love is...ignoring your phone when you are together. Unplug. What you allow will continue. Offline is peace of mind. Intercession is sowing a seed for power and inviting God to work in that person's life. Call on God and show loving-kindness to the people around you.

I declare: "I will be intentional about putting my phone down and engaging with people face-to-face."

JANUARY 22

One reason you may be resisting change is because you may be focusing on what you must give up instead of what you may gain. Doubting is part of the process. And do not expect others to understand it! It is your life, your God-given dreams, and your new choices. I did not wake up like this. I sought God *first*. I changed my thinking, I changed my daily habits, and I changed what and whom I listened to. I changed what I was reading. It has all been worth it. It may feel like a burden at first. But if you stay committed, all this will become a part of you, and this will be your daily therapy. Just remember when you told yourself you were not good enough! Build your faith, and your life will follow. Everything is hard before it is easy. The difference between wanting to change your life and achieving it...is *discipline*. Sacrifice now! And you will hear, "Well done, my faithful servant." Every day matters. Life starts at the end of your failures. If you always do what you have done, you will always get what you have always gotten. A prayer is a miracle in motion. Pray God's Word over all!

I declare: "I am disciplined in every area of my life."

JANUARY 23

Hang on. Let me overthink this. Do not trip and fall into your emotions now. Do not get mood poisoning! The next time the devil tries to get you stuck in your past, remind him of his future. Only Jesus can turn a test into a triumph. You are 100 percent forgiven. The poorest person on Earth is not the one without money but is the one without Jesus. If you have time to worry, you have time to pray. If you are overwhelmed today, it is a sign that you are spending less time with God and more time with what is going wrong. Sometimes, He stirs us out of comfortable situations to stretch us and cause us to build our faith and believe stronger in Him. Prayer is the most important conversation of your day. Pray before you overthink today. Start calling yourself: Healed, happy, whole, blessed, protected, and prosperous. Tell those situations how big your God is! Prayer goes against panic. Faith with prayer is your Wi- Fi; it is the power to connect you to God for your daily needs. Start right now speaking good things, and you will begin to see change. Your words have power.

I declare: "I will start my day with prayer every day."

JANUARY 24

Prayer is the jump start to a miracle. And it is your miracle.

The one thing that is standing between what you want, the will to try, and the faith in God to believe is you. There will be, you can count on this for sure, the nonbelievers. Nonbelievers will talk against your miracle. There will be haters. There will be doubters. And there will be you proving them wrong with your steadfast faith in God. You wake up every morning with yourself! You can either have faith results or excuses not to believe. But you cannot have both. It is very hard to beat a person of faith who never gives up. Do what is necessary to become who and what you want to achieve in this lifespan. When your weak mind asks, "Can I really do this?" reply *out loud* with, "*Absolutely, I can do all things through Christ who strengthens me.*" Do not wait until you feel motivated. Do it now. Your mind will catch up. Call me crazy, but I love crazy faith. What is my secret? It is called get up even when you don't feel like it, put on your positive pants, and get going. I never regret it when I do. But I always regret it when I do not. The best addiction is once you feel the faith working. And yes, it is powerful and possible.

I declare: "I 'can' do all things through Christ who strengthens me."

JANUARY 25

Today is the day I will ignore my excuses and go get it done. Make miracles happen, not excuses. I am not better than you; I need the daily pep talk too! Wake up! You only get this one life. Do not cry over mistakes. I am not perfect, but I am progressing. I am my solution. I am unstoppable in Jesus. To change your life, you must change your priorities. This will take everything you have got. There is no shortcut. Stay in "I will"! I love working on myself! What is my secret? I just get up and seek God very first thing! That's it! Be a prayer warrior. Not a worrier. Believe in the person you want to become. Be stronger than your excuses. Believe day after day, you are getting closer to your God-given goals. Visualize the person you want to be. And now work for it. Nothing good comes easy. Success starts with self-discipline. Focus right now on your goal, and do not look in any direction but ahead.

I declare: "I am getting closer and closer to my God-given goals."

JANUARY 26

Blame, complain, or obtain. When thinking about life, remind yourself no amount of guilt can change the past. You have greatness in you. Rise up and conquer. And next week, have this same attitude. You will never get results with half-hearted commitments. No time for drama either. We are all busy, so this cannot be an excuse to sacrifice your new goals. Big changes are made by taking small healthy habit-forming steps that greatly add up over time. You are a creature of your habits. Just do it. That is how you create your own new opportunities. Dust yourself off and find your courage. Ask yourself if what you are doing today is getting you closer to where you want to be tomorrow. If not, you have the power from the Holy Spirit to change that. Do not wait another day. Start listening to God's voice; He said you can. You were created fearfully and wonderfully made by Him.

I declare: "I am seeking new opportunities, and they will find me."

JANUARY 27

Find yourself! Stop people-pleasing. No finger-pointing, no pity party, and no looking pitiful. Stand and deal! I admire those who smile while they are going through tough stuff. What a beautiful saying, "I fell apart, and I survived." Your peace is important. Refresh your spirit daily by the power of the Holy Spirit. Silence is golden when no words can explain what is going on in your mind and soul. Seek the Lord first thing, review your positive affirmations, listen to faith-filled talks, read faith-filled books, and put in time for exercise weekly. These steps are a sure way to break the negative streak in your life. It is none of your business what others say about you, and minding your own business is a super plus. We are to be salt and light only. Jesus is not hiring any judges or critics; He holds that position. Salt and light—that is you. You cannot change someone who does not see a fault; stop trying. Listen to your heart, not opinions of others. By doing so, you will hear the voice of God. Be careful who you vent to, a listening ear or a running mouth. Thoughts and prayers are powerful but must be paired with change. We are what we believe. Stop worrying and start worshiping. Powerful. Rest is a weapon provided by God. The enemy hates it; he wants you stirred up and stressed out!

I declare: "But if from there you seek the LORD your God, you will find him if you seek him with all your heart and with all your soul" *(Deuteronomy 4:29, NIV).*

JANUARY 28

I promise no one is perfect. Value differences. I would rather surround myself with people who make mistakes; I promise no one is perfect. Value differences. I would then be around people who think they make none. My Bible does not have a verse about how love is demonstrated through critical comments and self-righteousness. Judging another person does not define them; you define yourself. Better to be a humble sinner than a self-righteous saint. Repeat over in your mind: I am quick to listen, slow to speak, and slow to anger. Enjoy the life God has given you. The Gospel is for the lost, to remove their despair. Self-righteousness has killed more people than smoking. Just because someone sins differently than you do does not make it right to judge. We are all sinners saved by grace. If we judge a book by its cover, we may miss out on an amazing story. We are always responsible for how we act. The only worst thing other than a proud sinner is a self-righteous saint. No one is sin free! No one. Love only grows by sharing. Humble ourselves under the mighty hand of God so that at the proper time, He will exalt you! It is necessary for us to control our emotions.

I declare: "I am quick to listen, slow to speak, and slow to anger. I am patient."

JANUARY 29

Signs of spiritual maturity: You do not force love; you live it. You forgive more. You respect differences. Your happiness does not depend on people; it comes from God. You do not judge; you show others patience. You love sharing the Word. You prefer to remain silent rather than to engage in foolishness. If you are tired, you learn to rest, not quit. Accept compliments gracefully but give all the glory to the Lord. Be concerned about others' comfort before yourself. Hold yourself to high standards always. Understand your own worth. Do favors for others without expecting anything in return. Savor the time. She has his heart, and he has hers. But their hearts belong to Jesus. A passion for God is the most attractive feature a person can possess. We shall be like trees planted by the rivers that bring forth good fruit. God gave me the love that the world could not offer me. A good person will tell you you're beautiful/handsome. A real spirit-filled person will make you believe it.

I declare: "I will thank the Lord for bringing me much peace and happiness in all I do."

JANUARY 30

The greatest relationships are built on teamwork, mutual respect, a healthy dose of admiration, and never-ending portion of grace and agape love. Do not forget...

- Most important in life—God.
- Most beautiful attire—smile.
- Greatest asset—faith.
- Most powerful force—love.
- Greatest weapon—prayer.

Love is sweet when it is new but even sweeter when it is true. Believe the best rather than the worst. Be with someone who will not ruin your mascara, only your lipstick. Love never fails. Pray with your other half. Be the greatest fan of each other's life. A true lady doesn't demand; she thanks. And a true man does not promise; he commits. Better together. When your human soul unites with the power of the Holy Spirit, it only can have one place, and that is death. The human soul must desire to cease to have its own way. You must crave God's will over yours, or you will lose every time! "May Your will be done in me, Lord."

I declare: "I will not live by what my flesh wants; I will live by what the Holy Spirit wants."

JANUARY 31

We will have what we believe. Are you believing good things? Believe that you have God's power in you. God is working. You do not marry someone you can live with. You marry someone you just cannot live without. But together, you will need faith in God, love, trust, lots of understanding, and respect always. No one can go back and have a brand-new start, but you can start right now to have the most brand-new ending. We may lose a battle or two, but we will not lose our faith or the will to keep going with our God. That is why faith is so important together. We will be okay because love is strong in the Lord. He keeps us close together and makes us stronger. We are a team! We make mistakes, and we promise to never give up on each other. Leave the past back there.

Communicate: talk about things. Appreciate the flaws that we all have. No emotional reasoning allowed. Blame is so harmful. If you are Holy Spirit-filled, it will teach your soul to remain in self-control. Your soul is your mind, your will, and your emotions. Stay spirit-controlled. Marriage is a thousand little things. Marriages last because people make choices: to keep it, to fight for it, to always be intentional, and to work on it. You must be loyal to one another. When someone does wrong, do not forget all the things they did right.

I declare: "I will leave the past behind me; I will not talk about it. I am going forward."

February

Keep your tongue from evil, and your lips from speaking deceit.

Psalm 34:13

Your words are powerful. Be careful what you speak.

FEBRUARY 1

You ask, "What will make me successful?" Your daily core habits will! Seek God, pray, and ask the Holy Spirit to give you a fresh download from heaven. It is called fresh new manna. Sit still and stay quiet with just you and the Lord. Turn off all the noise that surrounds you daily, and yes, that means your phone too. Avoid idle chatter and just be still. Wait on the Lord to renew your strength. Do not get disappointed or discouraged by naysayers saying things about you. Silence is the best reply to foolish talk. God designed you to have a creative position in this life. He created you on holy purpose. Just think about that for a moment. He has something that only you can do. Wow! Think of it this way. The God who created the heavens and the universe thought the earth needed someone special just like you. You were fearfully and wonderfully made by Him. Do not wait a second longer. Dig in the Word to see what He has in store for you this coming season. Learn not to listen to the bad news about you; that is not who you were destined to be. I see who you are in Christ, and you look marvelous! He is the author and the finisher of my faith.

I declare: "I will be still and wait on the Lord."

FEBRUARY 2

Never wait until tomorrow to start living life. Work on being your best self. No one was created to be you, and that is your power. Do not fear responsibility. Make each day special! Always keep in mind life is never perfect, but some moments are so special. Keep calm and know the King of kings. He is right there with you. Start up your positive affirmations and stick with them daily. That is how you chase your dreams...declaring the Word. This way, you will not stumble in the darkness. The God who blesses is greater than the blessing itself. Two types of people who will tell you that you will not make a difference in this world: those who are fearful to try and those who are fearful that you will succeed. Self-love and hard work will always earn you success. Stop doubting yourself; just work hard and "make it happen"! You will never feel satisfied by work only until you get plugged into the power of the Holy Spirit. God has a plan that can unfold right before your eyes. Just begin!

I declare: "I am fearfully and wonderfully made. There is not another 'me' that was created; I am unique."

FEBRUARY 3

Just keep breathing. Treat yourself. Everything you are going through is prepping you for your dream. I know even that situation you do not like! Do all things with love. Grateful for where I am at but very excited about where I am going. Do not waste that beautiful mind doing ugly things! Positive thoughts only. Hello, you are looking absolutely stunning today. To live your destiny, you must lose the fear of being wrong. We have tomorrow for a reason, with the thought the best is yet to come. Embrace your journey. Faith can move those moments that are in your way! Your life is not yours if you keep caring what others think! Surround yourself with people who inspire you, excite you, and are grateful for you! Just give me Jesus, and I know my plans will succeed! Start each day with a grateful heart. Life isn't perfect! Be bold to do what the ordinary fear.

I declare: "I will find ten things I am grateful for every day."

FEBRUARY 4

Our reaction to a situation literally has the power to change the situation itself. Communicate even when it is uncomfortable. Have faith that everything will work out. "Lord, I choose You, Your Word, and Your name above all!"

When others treat you poorly, keep being you. I am mighty in God. I am loved. I am valuable. I am strong in the Lord. I am bold and courageous. I am an empowering influence. I am directed by the Holy Spirit. I am an answer. You have victory through faith. Begin today to increase your faith. You must lay down selfishness; it must flee.

I declare: "I am going to stay confident and strong even if it's uncomfortable."

FEBRUARY 5

The happiest people are givers. The people in your life should be a source of reducing stress. Instead of complaining, get busy and create some new memories. Confidence is silent. I am currently under construction. I like closing for a Holy Spirit checkup! Recover and forgive and forget it. To God be the glory. Do not be fooled; success is falling nine times and getting up the tenth. Act the way you would want to be, and soon, you will be the way you think, talk, and act. You become what you believe.

Four things for success:

- pray,
- believe,
- think,
- work.

Without self-discipline, success is impossible, period. Success is quite often found in that pile of those mistakes. To know how to pray and wait is a great secret to your success. Praise God and stay humble.

I declare: "I believe what I prayed for is happening right now; I will wait patiently on the Lord."

FEBRUARY 6

My heart cannot point out enough to you that consistency is the most important key, especially on the days I do not feel motivated to work on my goals. I simply keep going. If you do not start today, what will make you motivated for tomorrow? God helps us handle our days when we seek Him first. I am believing that He will make my days useful, my evenings restful, my home and family peaceful, and all my efforts fruitful. Value your time. It is as important as your finances. You must know your weaknesses. That is where the enemy is going to attack. You will need a humble heart. I pray that God will use you to change lives. The enemy will want you to pay attention to your feelings; Jesus wants you to pay attention to His truth. The Word of God is alive, active, and sharper than any double-edged *sword*. One of the enemy's tricks of darkness is making us think that things are not okay with us. Even though God has already assured us that they are.

I declare: "God's got me. God will make sure that no man can get credit for what He's about to do."

FEBRUARY 7

Rule #1: *Never make God.* #2: Not my strength but His. Don't treat people as rude as they are to you; treat them as beautiful as you are. You are a part of God's marvelous plan. Wear clothes that show your heart. One day, you will wake up spiritually, and you will be glad you chose to wait on the plan of God. I surrender...I will trust Your plan, God, for my life. Before we ask God for another thing, let us thank Him for everything. You do not need anyone's approval; that is for insecure people. Pray; it causes miracles. Send someone a love letter this Valentine's Day. Life rooted in God stands firm. The perfect person in life is the one who makes you smile, loves God, and will put you first. I am always sure about what I don't want. You can create beautiful and handsome with your behavior, your actions, your words, and with your attitude. Believe when you are being tempted to give up! That means your supernatural breakthrough is just around the corner. Keep calm. And always keep your faith in God.

I declare: "I am ready. Even though God sends people into our lives to lead us closer to Him, the enemy also sends people to distract us. Pray for discernment."

FEBRUARY 8

Work on you, for you. May I ask why do you worry about what others think of you? Do you put more confidence in their opinions than you do your own? Today is going to be an amazing day...and here is why: because today, at least, you are you, and that is enough. Your only limit is your mind. Do not chase anyone. Know your worth. Save beautiful time for people who matter. Get rid of what is not you. Where your focus goes, your feet will follow. You were made for such a time as this. Let the One who created you define you. Now that is powerful. If you do not step forward, you will remain in the same place. How you love yourself will always teach others how to love you back. Be loyal in your relationships, take the extra steps, and when things feel tough, please do not quit. And soon, really soon, you will see why it was all worth your hard efforts. It is okay; it always will take baby steps to climb the highest mountain. Things take time. You owe this to yourself. Do not be just eye candy, be soul food.

I declare: "If anyone is in Christ, he is a new creation. The old has passed away; behold, the new has come."

FEBRUARY 9

Just remember, someone loves everything you hate about yourself. God created you amazing and on purpose. Self-love is a beautiful medicine for your soul. Look back at where you came from. You are allowed to be both a masterpiece and a work in progress. Do not let others pull you into their storm. You pull them into your peace. When you are on a high road, you will receive criticism from those on the lower road. They are reporting from the level they are on. You will win if you do not hate on anyone and just stay in your lane. Zipper *up*! God is promoting you to a new place and a new season. Never put your time into the hands of the ungrateful. Your attitude is contagious. Never stop praying for the best of everyone. That is how you fight your battles. We love because He loved us first. You are good enough, smart enough, and strong enough.

I declare: "Above all, love each other deeply because love covers over a multitude of sins."

FEBRUARY 10

Declare: I radiate unconditional love. I allow the Holy Spirit to work on me for healthy relationships. Stay true to your frequency from the supernatural Holy Spirit. We give too many people the power to lower our standards. Train your mind to be strong from the Word of God. This will always be stronger than your emotions. If you follow emotions, you will lose every single time. If you do not correct emotions when they upset you, you will never learn how to operate out of your higher nature. Stay focused. Try a different approach today, drop it, leave it, let it go. Let God continue to fight your battles. To find yourself, lean on Him more. Your two powerful warriors are patience and time. Look for your passion; that is your authentic self. That is the one you lost beneath other people's needs. Rebuild yourself in private. Life humbles you as you age. Feel the feeling, but do not become the emotion. Witness it and quickly release it. Be valuable, not available. My mission in life is to thrive. It is a beautiful thing to be able to stand tall and declare; I fell apart, but glory to God, I am a survivor. There are hidden blessings in every single struggle.

I declare: "I radiate unconditional love. I allow the Holy Spirit to work on me for healthy relationships. I fell apart, but glory to God, I am a survivor."

FEBRUARY 11

Just a short reminder, you cannot please everyone. Stop trying. Calm yourself, and the storm will pass. Detox your contact list. Detox your mind. Be kind even on your bad days.
Start doing what you were born to do. Start stepping towards
your God-given calling. The most important days of your life
are when you are born and the day you find out why! God had
a specific and special purpose in mind when He created you.
Your purpose is to make a difference in this life. You matter.
Your voice matters. Your testimony is important. Your dreams
will impact. You came here with a purpose. You had a purpose
before anyone had an opinion about you. Think about that,
even on your darkest day. Declare: I have this fire in me. I have
a purpose. I refuse to stay stuck. Purpose is the reason for this
journey orchestrated by God. Pursue purpose. Your only limit is you. The meaning of life is to find your gift! Crave God's
Word. He is making a masterpiece out of you.

*I declare: "I have this fire in me. I have a purpose. I refuse to stay
stuck."*

FEBRUARY 12

Some people do not change, and you do not want to forgive.

Release others from your punishment, and do not celebrate their failures. Whoever keeps his mouth and tongue quiet keeps his soul from trouble. Never again will I confess defeat, for God always causes me to triumph in Him. Never again will I confess weakness, for the Lord is my strength. This is called taming the tongue. Nothing others do or say is because of you. What others say and do is an insight of their own heart, their own dream. Speak with integrity to others and over yourself. What others do is always because of themselves, do not take it personally. The Holy Spirit always comforts me and teaches me, guides me, warns me, and keeps me from harm. Reset. Restart. No response is a response and a very powerful one. There is nothing classier than showing grace and forgiveness to someone who does not deserve it. Write someone a note of encouragement. It is powerful!

I declare: "I am always comforted by the Holy Spirit; I sit quietly and seek Him."

FEBRUARY 13

I refuse to allow negative thinking to ruin my day. A few nice words can help others a lot more than you think. The sign of a beautiful person is that they always see beautiful in others. There is a message in the way others treat you, stop and just listen. I believe miracles are good people with kind hearts. You just may be a reason someone believes in the goodness of others! He heals the wounds of every shattered heart. Everything that is broken is in His hands. Declare: I am deeply loved by the Creator of the universe. Prayer is the cure for a broken heart. Self-care is not selfish. I am putting my life in order. It is not that I cannot; I am making healthier choices not to... Mind... body... and soul. When you do what God wired you to do, it brings glory to Him. Hello. You are looking healthy today. I speak and think positively. Get into the Word. The Holy Spirit has a download from heaven just for you. Depending on Him alone!

I declare: "I am deeply loved by the Creator of the universe."

FEBRUARY 14

Fear is a liar. It is not about a gift! It is all about faithfulness, trustworthiness, and unconditional love that matters the most. Love is a learned behavior. Your time means more than a gift. Do not tear down. Build up! The God of that mountain top is still the God of the valley. It is now that time to gather strength from the Source of all strength. Give a piece of your heart away today. Changing the world we live in, one love letter at a time. Bring back the love letter; it is tender, it is your handwriting, and you can make it as romantic as you would like. It is a step up from receiving a text. For God gave us a spirit not of fear but of power, love, and self-control. Celebrate life. Believe in yourself. Blessed. Be the present. You are powerful, beautiful, brilliant, and brave. Do not overthink things. Write that love letter! Love only gets old if you let it. I am a pencil in the hand of God.

I declare: "I do not fear; I walk in love, power, and self-control."

FEBRUARY 15

Stop letting your emotions make all your decisions. Do not repay evil with evil or insult with insult. You were called to repay evil with a blessing so you may inherit a blessing. When it is not in God's plan, you cannot force it. But when it is the plan of God, nothing can stop it. You cannot control how others see you or even think of you. And you will always have to be comfortable with that right there. Love is something you become because He loved us first. No matter what you are going through, one day, you will look back and see how the struggles changed you for the better. Let the future be your motivation. Watch God's next move. I have to keep reminding myself God has a huge plan. Trust Him now. God will speak to you; just listen.

I declare: "I decree and declare God has the plan for my life, and I will follow Him."

FEBRUARY 16

When times get tough, get going and stop tripping on your own negative words. Stop speaking about what you see that is not good. Words hold the key to your future and your freedom. Write down everything you are thinking right now. Will your own words bless your future or curse it? I have often made a list of great things that I want to see happen over my life. When I backed it up with God's promises and changed the way I was speaking, I started seeing positive results. Change the way you speak, and you will change your attitude. As for me and my household, we will serve the Lord with gladness. If God is for me, who can be against me? I can do all things through Christ who strengthens me. The battles in my life belong to the Lord. No weapon formed against me shall prosper in Jesus' name. I am set free. I am renewed. I am delivered. I am blessed. I am living my best life. I am in the best physical shape ever. I have a great attitude. This is the day the Lord has made. I will rejoice and be glad.

I declare: "My words will bless my future."

FEBRUARY 17

Do you know what your worst enemy is? Overthinking! Overthinking creates problems that do not even exist. Then you start speaking about what you are thinking, and now you must fight off that depression. The best way to ward off these negative emotions is to quickly replace your thoughts with the powerful, two-edged sword, the Word of God. There are 365 scriptures against fear. One for every day of the week because God foreknew we all would struggle with the spirit of fear. I do know this is not an easy task, and still, some will not believe that replacing your fearful thoughts with the Word of God works! But that is okay; at one time, I did not believe it worked either. So, we are all forgiven with this spirit of unbelief. Start today and right away kick off your new day with your new powerful, supernatural, paranormal, preternatural words from the holy Word. It is so powerful and priceless that I just cannot leave home without it. Do not wait one more day. We need Him more and more! I admit it; I just cannot go through this life without being covered by the Word of God!

I declare: "God is not the spirit of fear; He is of love, 'power,' and a sound mind!"

FEBRUARY 18

What do you do when you have disagreements? Do you examine yourself to see what you are thinking? Do you encourage yourself in the Lord to trust Him and do good? The first step is the hardest in the right direction. God has a silent reward just for you when you rise above the rest and always do your best. Working out of your higher nature, although uncommon, is rewarding. We teach our children by example as they watch us handle simple situations. This is so amazing and powerful. All your moves in life are so important and life-changing. Your family is so worth it. Words, actions, and promises are related to your integrity. What are you teaching your children? Show more of you! Every day, every word and every promise reveals to others your true self. So, what are you doing with your life? Breaking promises? Breaking dreams? Or are you building up others and creating dreams for them and yourself? You are what you say and do. Let us, together, make life worth living one day at a time! Honor God and your home life. Build up one another. Live life on purpose. Be who God created you to be. Give it all you have got. Be brave and be beautiful on purpose. Daily prayer and Bible reading are essential to our growth. At one time, I didn't think it worked. I was wrong!

I declare: "I will focus and work out of my higher nature."

FEBRUARY 19

Every one of us faces tough times, but we do not have to let tough times torment us. These tough moments will refine you, not define you. I have learned that God uses every problem for building our character. In some of my darkest times, I grew so confident in the Lord and stepped out on faith for Him to move, which is where I began to trust God in new ways. I had to let go and just let God take over. Rise above the distractions and face the what-ifs and change your thinking to His Word and stand on the promise that you want to see. Greater is He that is in you than he that is in the world. He loves us if we are weak or strong. Stop tormenting yourself with a negative mindset. When life gets tough, check to see if you're following God or yourself. You may be facing a hard challenge, but He is right with you. It costs a price to follow Him, but it will cost a whole lot more not to. The Lord is my Shepherd. Trust the Holy Spirit; He will give you power.

I declare: "I choose to walk through my battles with the Lord and not be moved by them."

FEBRUARY 20

Forgive. Letting go is not about getting anyone off the hook; it is for your total freedom. Negative energies cannot stay around me. When you forgive, you heal. The weak cannot forgive; forgiveness is a beautiful attribute of the strong. Forgiveness heals. Unforgiving is an acid that will harm your vessel. I had some strong issues with my younger self, but I was young, and I forgave her. Forgiveness is my freedom. I do not even think about forgiveness; I just do it. Forgive just as God has forgiven you. Love keeps no record of being wronged. Your inner peace can only be opened when you practice forgiveness. Never go to sleep angry. Do not hold grudges. The worst thing we can ever do when we are treated unfairly is get a sour attitude because someone else just cannot be sweet. Rise above it. Forgive even if you do not feel like it until it becomes a beautiful habit. This is how you grow and get crazy blessings. Forgiveness unlocks doors. Forgiveness sets you free. Forgive to let go. You must forgive yourself. Jesus forgives even that.

I declare: "I choose to forgive so I may live in peace at all times."

FEBRUARY 21

If your goal is personal growth, it is time to reflect and to bloom! Select your thinking and speaking the exact way you select your clothes. The only thing you should be controlling is your own mind and words. Be thankful for the bad things that might have gone unnoticed, for they opened your eyes to the good you want to be. Before you were not paying attention. Your diet? It is not only what you select to eat. It is what you are watching, what you are reading, who you are hanging out with, and how you dress. Be mindful of all things; it will help you physically, mentally, and spiritually. Declare: I am the picture of well-being. Every one of my cells is filled with wholeness and wellness. I am directed by God. How fast we age is a bit of a surprise. I always knew it would happen, but it flies by so fast! Working hard for something you love is called passion. Patience is power. Passion is love. You can't pour from an empty cup. Take care of yourself first. Our attitude is the color that paints your life beautiful or gloomy! Do not feel unsupported; He is always faithful and by your side!

I declare: "I am the picture of well-being. Every one of my cells is filled with wholeness and wellness. I am directed by God."

FEBRUARY 22

Never look down at others...only if you are helping them up. You have a choice: pain of discipline or the pain of your regret. Stop being controlled by people and your past. Your world is not falling apart; it is falling into God's perfect plan. Keep your eyes on the cross, not your storms. Train your mind to stay calm even in that storm. If you are right about a situation, stay humble and quiet. Sit back and just observe. Everything does not need an opinion. And the peace of God, which surpasses all understanding, will guard your hearts and your minds in Jesus. He reached down from on high and took hold of me. He drew me out of the deep waters. Thank you for not giving up on me. No disaster can overtake you; no plague can come near your dwelling; for He shall give His angels charge over you to keep you in all your ways. He is perfect in all His ways.

I declare: "I am blessed to be a blessing."

FEBRUARY 23

Have fun, even if it is not what everyone else is doing.

It is funny how day by day goes by fast, and nothing really changes until you look back and everything is different. Daily we meet no ordinary people in life. Just like the sunrise does not even care if you watch it or not, it still rises daily. Keep that childlike heart with that grown-up head. Our life with God does not immune us from situations but will give us peace in situations. You are what you believe you are. Declare: Today, I am going to make everything around me beautiful; this will be my life. We read to realize we are not alone in life's situations. We love because He first loved us. I want to be that person who trusts that God has the plan even when I cannot see it and even when I do not understand. God gives happiness to those who can give it away to others.

I declare: "Today, I am going to make everything around me beautiful; this will be my life."

FEBRUARY 24

Human life is a long story of man searching to find happiness other than seeking the Lord, which will make him very satisfied and so happy. If you are having a bad thought about yourself, tell it to flee and leave because it is not from God. We will not get disappointed by comparison if we are consumed with our purpose. You do not need to have it all figured out to move on. Just do it. What draws others together as great friends is that we share the same truth. An old-fashioned heart is timeless and holds timeless love. Pray for that! Love is eternal. Everything that has no eternal value will be worthless later! What we do for Christ is eternal. Friendships are born the minute we say to another heart, "Oh, I thought I was the only one who did that!" Be real. Stay humble. Stay honest and loving. Declare: I choose to make the rest of my life the best of my life. No one *can* cast the first stone. We are all sinners saved by grace; it is a pure, beautiful gift from God...not from ourselves. Stay real! Repeat after me: "My current problem is not my destination." Constantly change yourself. No feelings; try just thinking. Frame your world with the Word!

I declare: "I choose to make the rest of my life the best of my life."

FEBRUARY 25

Be so positive that negative people do not want to be near you. As you seek to be a Kingdom thinker, you need to know what matters most to the King! Right thinking is vital to the Kingdom. Your calling? It is bigger than you are. It is all about the people you are called to impact. Repeat that to yourself. Before you lay down those huge prayers, you must first lay down your opinions of others. We are to live in that place called more than enough. When you pray, think of all those no one prays for. You are a child of God. I have realized that everything, every single thing, in this life is fleeting, and only God is eternal. You were not an accident. You were deliberately planned and gifted by the King of kings. Declare: God designed me. Created me. Blesses me. Heals me. Defends me. Forgives me. Loves me. Complaining proves nothing, only that you can hear the voice of the enemy.

I declare: "God designed me. Created me. Blesses me. Heals me. Defends me. Forgives me. Loves me."

FEBRUARY 26

What is my purpose in this fallen world? I dedicate my writings to the Lord who saved me from myself. Trust in the Lord and *do good*! Delight yourself in the Lord, and He shall give you the desires of your heart. God has so much more just for you. You can make plans, but it is the Lord who determines your steps. Go ahead and express your emotions to God alone. Say it to Him. God is going before you right now to lead you. He is also behind you to protect you. Do not worry, for He is on the sides of you to guide and guard you. Jesus be a fence. He is preparing the way. Keep walking. He is doing 10,000 things in your life that you cannot see. Trust Him. Pray in the power of the Holy Spirit. That is your prayer language. *Abba*, Father, I declare that today is *my day*. Speak blessings over your home. Rest because you just cannot pour from an empty cup. Come, Holy Spirit, renew my mind, body, and soul. Pray for your role as a parent. Pray that you will be quick to forgive. Pray for your relationships with your family.

I declare: "Today is 'my day.'"

FEBRUARY 27

Your setback may not be your fault, but your healing is all your responsibility. Overthinking does absolutely nothing except kill your joy and happiness. Interrupt that unhappiness with the spirit of gratitude. Your circle in life should be a safe place of reducing anxiety, not adding to it. Right now, let go of every thought that is not training your brain to stay positive. Pain changes people. And anxiety does not come up from thinking about your future. It pops up by us wanting to control it. Wake up happy. Life is a gift and is denied by many. Let this sink in: it took nine months to form you. Do not let anyone break you. God is my strength and my power, and He will make my way perfect. Worship is, "I *declare*..." of war against everything that says God cannot. I choose to worship. The Lord is faithful.

I declare: "I will let go of 'all' people, situations, and things that cause anxiety."

FEBRUARY 28

You can rise above anything. You can completely change yourself. You are not stuck. Learn to stay humble. I know life is hard. Six months of focus, great habits, and staying disciplined with much hard work can put you five years ahead in life. This is called the power of discipline. It takes time to heal. Take chances. Stay filled with self-love...you make better choices that way. Always tell others how important they are to you. I just want to make a difference. Strong people never really have an easy past. I know God has amazing plans. Ask for guidance and direction. Always have the faith to believe that something wonderful is about to happen. Revive the peace in me. I pray that every battle that is draining you physically and emotionally comes to an end in the name of Jesus. So far, you have survived 100 percent of your worst days. You are doing great!

I declare: "I will sit in silence and listen to God's voice and nudges for His guidance and direction."

FEBRUARY 29

Most Christians will not hear the voice of God because they decide they are not going to do what He says anyways. You can be sure when the Holy Spirit enters a man, he cannot live like the world.

"As this year progresses, mold me and shape me until I think just like You, Lord." Listen to no man who will not listen to God. There are two ways to influence others: you can manipulate or inspire. Do not let anyone ruin your day. Your discipline will dictate your success over all! I adore positive people. Do not ignore a truth for temporary happiness; it is a trick from the devil. No advice needed; maybe deliverance. One of my goals is to never let myself fall. Dear God, I am placing each day in the palm of Your capable hands. Life has been full of lessons. If there is anything in your way, your heart will feel it! You can create a new season, a new breakthrough! The Gospel can make the way! If it does not matter in five years, do not spend more than five minutes being upset about it! Everything in your life is a decision you will make. What you speak and the actions you take all begin in your mind! So as a new day begins, rejoice and expect *great expectations!*

I declare: "I will remain positive in every situation and with everyone I meet."

March

Kings take pleasure in honest lips; they value the one who speaks what is right.

Proverbs 16:13 (NIV)

Your words are powerful. Be careful what you speak.

MARCH 1

Get into the daily habit of asking yourself, "Does this support the positive, powerful life I am trying to create?" You have one life. How do you want to live it? Build up: Not tear down. Encourage: Not discourage. Remove the toxic things from life. Success is preparation and opportunity. Attract people. Be an example. And we know for those who love God, all things work together for good. Encourage each other and build each other up. Above all else, love each other deeply. Do not worry; just *pray*. Worry about nothing. Pray about everything. Talk to God. Be willing to create the life that you have the desire to live on purpose.

I declare: "I am supporting the positive, powerful life I am creating."

MARCH 2

In life, I hope we all make it! You are you. I am I. Life is about inspiring others. We can make ourselves strong, or we can make ourselves miserable. It takes the same amount of work. Life is a very special gift. Keep putting out blessings. I just want to spend the rest of my life encouraging others. Live your life and forget about your age. No complaining; just appreciate the life you have. Being positive is called leadership. I am simply trying to be better than I was yesterday. See the glow in others and treat them as if that is all you see in them! *Powerful!* It is never okay to be cruel. Kindness is used by the strong in the spirit realm. You are enough. Grace means all your past mistakes are serving a purpose instead of serving you shame. Trust God's grace. Joy is a choice. Cultivate kindness. Do not be so hard on you. Make generosity part of your growth strategy. I pray we all make it!

I declare: "I am inspiring others; in turn, I am inspired."

MARCH 3

Do not be the person chasing empty paths; it will not profit or deliver one good thing. Watch out for hoaxes that will try to steal and destroy the plan of God over your life. Yep, people-pleasing is one of them. When you chase an empty lifestyle, it will damage you later. Be smart. There is no better new start than the rebirth of your heart to God. Fame, wealth, fortune, title, or status quo will never satisfy you like Jesus can. An empty space is an empty space. Being born again will change your whole life to a new you (John 3:3). From darkness to His marvelous light. Keep praying to God, who gives new beginnings. God longs to bless His creation. God desires us to live above circumstances. Everything is in His eternal plan; there are no surprises to God. Who's in charge? You know who is: He sits in the heavens and scoffs at our enemies. The earth is His footstool. The name above all names. Blessed Redeemer. Lord of all. He is the Messiah.

I declare: "Show me the way. I will build my life upon Your Word. I will build my heart upon Your love. I will not be shaken. There is no one like You. Open the eyes of my heart. I will build my trust in You."

MARCH 4

I owe God everything! If you are in a place where God is all you have, then you have all you need. Do you feel like what you need is impossible? Well, Jesus changed my whole life when I was down too impossible. There is a reason! They did not leave you; God moved them for a greater reason. Always put God first! If you just can place your beautiful heart in God's hands, He will place your heart where it is supposed to be. God is a necessity to your lifeline. Put the armor of God on daily. When you do this by faith, you are telling the devil that he must go through Jesus to get you (Ephesians 6:10–20). Put God first and watch amazing things happen. No matter what you face in life, do not let go of God's hand!

I declare: "I will place my heart in God's hands."

MARCH 5

Refuse to worry. Declare: I am patient. I am kind. I do not envy. I do not dishonor others. I am not proud. I am not self-seeking. I am not easily angered. I keep no records of wrongdoing. I do not delight in evil, but I do rejoice in truth. I always protect. I always trust. I always hope. I always persevere. This is the Word of God. Overcome evil with good. Normal people do not go around destroying other human beings. If someone wants to be a part of your life, they will show it positively. Always stay in hope. Make your requests be known to God! The meaning of life is to give life a meaning. Your power is through the name of Jesus to be an overcomer. *Magnify* the name of Jesus. Don't focus on yourself; instead, appreciate the power in His name! In the name of Jesus!

I declare: "I am patient. I am kind. I do not envy. I do not dishonor others. I am not proud. I am not self-seeking. I am not easily angered. I keep no records of wrongdoing. I do not delight in evil, but I do rejoice in truth. I always protect. I always trust. I always hope. I always persevere."

MARCH 6

Discipline your mind! And guess what? It is not easy, but you are worth it. If you are not worth tempting, you are not worth much. If someone has hurt you, pray for them. And then let it go...completely. Your words mean absolutely nothing when your actions are the complete opposite. God is fighting for you even if you cannot see it. That rejection only exists in the battlefield of your mindset. We must be mature enough to understand that sometimes, we have toxic traits too. It is not always the other person. Be still. The Lord will fight for you if you truly stay in trust of Him. Do not lose yourself. Practice self-love daily with your affirmations. Run as fast as you can towards God. We accept the love we think we deserve. God is all love! If you had enough time to do the wrong, you had enough time to think about it. If you are reading this, I pray you find strength in God to get through what you are going through. Be a coach to yourself; you serve a King; you cannot be one! Prepare your mind for action.

I declare: "My actions will reflect my higher nature."

MARCH 7

For the rest of the week, go all in with the mode: spiritually, mentally, and physically. Make stuff happen. Excuses are from the workshop of the devil; ignore them. Rolling around in your bed will not achieve anything. Be your own coach. I am fighting for a better me and a better life. You will run this day or ruin it; the choice is yours. Work hard, stay humble, and let success be your noise. It is not about being the best. It is about being a better you. Blame, complain, or obtain? So, it is a bad day? And you are going to let this kill your progress and confidence? It is you against you. Pause if you must! It is simple; do not stop. May you walk by faith and not by sight. May you live by God's promises. God is involved in directing your steps. Declare: The Lord is stirring me up today. He is filling me with strength, power, and His wisdom to change me into a better me. I refuse to quit. I will not get distracted or discouraged. He is faithful to complete the good work He has started. I will not let anything disturb me. I have peace, joy, and patience. I lack nothing. "You, Lord, are my firm foundation. That is enough for me."

I declare: "Thank You, Lord, for stirring me up today and filling me with Your strength and power."

MARCH 8

Think of all the wonderful things God has met just for you!

Remind yourself today of all His works so you cannot stay in doubt! Life is about getting better every single day! Look for improvements! Our life is what our thoughts make it or break it. What you allow in your thinking is what will continue, good or bad. If you want to be trusted, live honestly. Time will always discover truth. People are as beautiful as they care and as they share. Always, always do your best, even if no one gives you credit. Those thoughts shape your vision. The Lord Himself goes before you. He will never leave you or forsake you. Do not be afraid. Do not be discouraged. This life has no remote. If you want a change, get up and change it.

I declare: "I am doing my best today, no matter what my circumstances are."

MARCH 9

Today is the beginning of the rest of your life. So, what is your plan? Think before you respond. Do not just react. Get serious about living your best life. Life goes by so fast. Plan that family vacation. Go on a date night with your spouse. Give that child attention, especially the one that reminds you of you. Go visit your family; they will not be there forever. I want to live a life with no regrets. Those desires you have in your heart are placed there by our heavenly Father. Pray about living the dream on purpose. Declare: I have strong spiritual discernment. I will be an awesome blessing today wherever I go. I am directed by the Holy Spirit. I am an empowering influence for God. I am a beautiful blessing. This is going to be a fantastic day. I have wisdom, understanding, and God's grace wherever I go. I believe there is a specific time for everything. I am striving always to be a better me. I have a purpose. Safeguard that mind against negativity: it is your responsibility!

I declare: "I have strong spiritual discernment. I have a positive mindset. I am an awesome blessing today wherever I go."

MARCH 10

Do you seriously think God will not use you? He can do exceedingly and abundantly above all that we ask or think. Sometimes, God stays silent until we are ready to listen to Him. Meanwhile, the enemy will also try to limit your prayer time. Why? Because that devil knows your praying will kick him out of your life so you can be used by God. God will not move in your life because you are struggling. He moves in when you *pray*! Satan will target your mind with lies to make you go against God's Word. Your weapon is the inspired Word of God! Open your Bible. You are in that storm because God wants to show you that He is the only shelter. It is called "Godfidence" instead of self-confidence. We are the church. Enjoy every moment.

I declare: "I am listening to God today, not my own thoughts or feelings."

MARCH 11

You are different than others. You are unique. And so are your children. If you desire others to get along and love you, start by loving them first. Do not limit yourself by thinking people should be just like you. We all have different fingerprints on purpose, designed by God! When someone is damaged, do not damage them more. Pray for them and love them. The world will help damage you. Be careful what you say and do next! Drop the "l" from the "world" and seek the *Word* over your damaged situations. The "L" stands for lies and labels what the world and others say about you. Do not take them to heart. God loves you and will help you get on the right road to success over all your situations. Cry out to the Lord. Ask Him what the next step is. Open your Bible and be careful not to react but to respond with patience and love. Think about this: When we go shopping at the flea market, we know what to look for before we purchase it, which makes it valuable. Jesus knows and helps us look beyond our problems and helps us to see the value in those who are damaged. Restore them with gentleness. He has great plans for your children, so encourage them today. Lift them up in prayer.

I declare: "I will love others today as God would love them. I will not judge them."

MARCH 12

The more negative you are, the longer it will take to turn yourself around! Stop being led by your situations. Do not be led by emotional words or choices either. No fear or worry. Do not stay depressed! Would you like things different? Listen to God's voice: peace, love, encouragement, brightens, leads, reassuring, still. Not Satan's voice: worry, fear, condemnation, rushes, fearful, discouraging, obsessive. Slow down and take a deep breath. Stay calm and pray before you leap! Do not be stressed; it is a trick of the enemy. Satan cannot read our thoughts, but he can hear those negative, fearful, defeating, nasty words you are speaking. *Praise* God out loud instead. That is how you fight your battles. Does the devil know what you're thinking? No. Is it God's voice or the enemies? God's voice will always bring you clarity and bring you closer to God. The enemy's voice unleashes controlling spirits. Speak *life*. To see new plans and to see all things differently, seek God for answers. New plans, new life. Most unhappiness is due to listening to yourself!

I declare: "I will be led by God's voice and wait patiently until I hear from Him. If it's not of peace, it's not of God."

MARCH 13

If you dare to believe, nothing will stop you but *you*. You have the time. You just need to make it a priority. Have courage. Never lose hope. Surround yourself with winners; the conversation is different. No one ever wrote down a plan to be negatively filled, broken, lazy, or out of shape. That is what happens when you do not have a plan! Do whatever it takes to achieve new goals. Declare: I am walking firmly on solid ground. I am equipped with faith from God. I am living victoriously with the sword of the Spirit, your Word of power, as I go about my new day. God had me in mind before I was born. I am confident that the Holy Spirit will reveal my purpose to me. My favorite activity is minding my own business. I believe God can change our minds. Be transformed by the renewing of your mind!

I declare: "I am walking firmly on solid ground. I am equipped with faith from God."

MARCH 14

Your big dreams will not work unless you do. Watch your habits. Stay in prayer. Confess your daily affirmations. Read your faith-filled books. Listen to faith-filled messages. If the door does not open, it is simple; it is not your door. Doubting is part of the process and makes you question why you are doing all this work. "Lord, give me patience." And then it happens, one day, you wake up, and you are in a beautiful season. Your mind is powerful and positive. You have great peace. Your mind is crystal clear. Your soul is calm. The Lord will direct your steps. He does delight in every detail of your life. Though you may stumble, you will not fall. For the Lord holds you by your hand. Keep asking. Keep searching. Keep knocking. My never again list, I cannot fear. Doubt. Be weak. Be defeated! Why? For I can do all things through Christ who strengthens me. Opportunity is a visitor, do it now!

I declare: "I will pay close attention to my habits and break the ones that don't work."

MARCH 15

Here is a thought. Do not get defensive; just say, "Thanks for letting me know your thoughts." You cannot win with an argumentative, negative-thinking person. Your mindset is all about how you are from the very moment you wake up until the moment you lay your head down. Who you are, what you think, what you say, and how you feed—all starts with you. Maturity is teaching yourself to start your day off with peace of mind, respect, value, and beautiful self-worth. Your intention is everything. It is just not necessary to react to everything you hear or notice. How you spend your day and time and mindset is your life. Difficult situations are never worth losing yourself over. Be the person who helps encourage others without telling the world you did. People will join you because of a great attitude. And people will leave because of a poor attitude. If you cannot be positive, then at least be quiet. No word from God will ever fail. And this is all part of His beautiful plan kept by the power of our mighty God!

I declare: "I will be quiet if I do not have something positive to say."

MARCH 16

Nobody could ever replace you. No one compares to you.

Be grateful for where you are at. But stay excited for where you are going. Just because you took longer than others does not mean you have failed. Embrace the hurt. Just keep believing in yourself. Get up early. Start your day with prayer. Smile and do what you must do. Complain, remain. Ignore others' negative opinions. Stop apologizing for being positive. What seems impossible today will one day become your warm-up. Pause if you must, but do not stop. Do not remind yourself how impossible it may be. Every positive step brings you closer to your possible goal. No weapon formed against me will prosper; no enemy scheme against me will succeed. I live and breathe and serve powerfully under the Almighty God.

I declare: "I am making a list of ten things I am grateful for every day."

MARCH 17

"Lord, send out laborers for Your harvest. The laborers are few."

Daily, we must pray that we can deny our flesh. People say I am doing this "Jesus thing" too seriously. Well, I do not think so. He took me pretty seriously when He gave His whole life up for all my sins to give me eternal life. He renewed my mind. He gave me new insight and wisdom to live my best life. I have no regrets. I was busted and broken. I needed a Savior. He is my rock. I stepped out of my comfort zone and became a mighty woman of God. For God did not give us the spirit of fear but of a mighty power, agape love, and a beautiful, peaceful mind. Not of my own strength but from the Holy Spirit, I prayed to the Lord. He answered me, and He freed me from *all* my fears. Dying to self daily. I have no greater joy than to hear my family walking in God's grace. To me, that is the best success you can ever have. It is eternal *success*. Nothing that has happened to you is a surprise to God. God will still get you to where you are supposed to be. Trust Him!

I declare: "I will repeat daily; I am a child of God; I am the righteousness in Christ Jesus."

MARCH 18

You are either going to wake up inspired or intimidated by this day. No matter what, get up. Show up. And never give up. Remember, it is not your age, gender, or financial situation that helps you to be successful. It all starts with your mindset. See what you need. You do not need others to believe in you. You need to believe in yourself and believe in the Lord and His will for your life. You are a warrior. I had no choice. I had to change or live doomed. Do not play games with yourself. It is a hard truth. You are loved by God. Turn down your emotions and hustle up and surrender to God. You are fully known and loved by Him. Surround yourself with believers, dreamers, and doers. No matter what you do, every small achievement will soon be one amazing success story for you to share. You can find me somewhere in between inspiring others, working on myself, dodging negativity, and seeking the God I know so He can make a way. Know your worth. Stop getting distracted by things or people that have nothing to do with your goals. Never ever run back to what broke you. You must feel the love within before you can share it. You cannot do any of the above on your own; you need the power of the Holy Spirit. I admit that I cannot do any of it without Him. Let whoever think whatever; you just keep getting better.

I declare: "I can. I will."

MARCH 19

You truly grow when you believe that God is good, does good, and works all things out for our good and for His glory. Do not let today be a waste of waking up. But first, seek ye the Kingdom. Sure, my life is not perfect, but my God is. If you are sad, add more positive scripture affirmations and attack this day. Being positive is not about being perfect. When you are fearless, you are being positive. Do not let anyone dull your sparkle. Beauty starts in your head, not in the mirror. God constantly tells me, "I got you like I always do." Abandon the world and run to God. Life was never meant to be lived without God. I loved my life and made all my own choices and ended up in the biggest mess I could ever ask for. God reached down and rescued me. The best way to keep the enemy out is to keep Christ in. I am complete in Him. Do not underestimate the power of consistency and desire. Every morning you have two choices: continue to sleep and dream or jump up and chase your dreams. When you wake up early, you are telling yourself you are a leader. This will boost your mentality. Then work on your spiritual being and seek God to kick up your attitude. Jump on this even if you do not want to, and you will be glad you did.

I declare: "Give yourself grace to do what you can, where you are, with what you have."

MARCH 20

One year will go by, and it will take the same amount of time whether you make a change or not. We pay a high price for living low! Do not be fooled. We do not get away with anything. Today, make that hard decision to do something amazing for the Lord. If you keep on complaining, you do not have a solution. When you feel like stopping, look around, there is a little person watching who wants to be just like you. I am satisfied with many things in my life, but nothing compares to being a parent. The bravest thing you can ever do is show your genuine love. God's love is enough to save you from operating out of your lower self. Sometimes, it is so difficult to stick to working out of your higher nature. But I tell myself daily, "Don't quit." Suffer now and stick it out and live the rest of your life as a champion for God. Be so good that others just cannot ignore you. Do not say one word. Let your hard efforts and good work make all the noise. Live your life around opportunities and optimistic people. Do not waste time; it is valuable. Stand for what you believe in. Daily, you must spend time alone with God. When you take that first step and see and feel the difference, you will never stop. *Focus.*

I declare: "I will allow God's grace to shine through my ability to love others with sincere patience, gratitude, and acceptance."

MARCH 21

God, help me to trust Your plan.

The very first thing you should know about others is that they are not you. This should help you with your relationships. If you listen carefully, others will tell you what kind of people they are. Once you have accepted your own flaws, you can go to work on yourself, not your neighbor. The price of discipline is always less than the pain of that regret. Your limit is created by what you think you cannot do. Only fools believe they cannot *change*. You are a warrior. The hardest thing in life is to know what bridge to burn so you can follow the cross. You must want to succeed. A Boaz man displays the character and grace of Jesus and covers his Ruth with Christ's unconditional love. A Boaz is a blessing to Ruth. He showers her with kindness and grace where there has been none before. Ruth recognizes when she has received favor and does not take it for granted. Look for a woman who prays for you. One who will speak to you like a king. Boaz will always be a gentleman. A Boaz prays for his Ruth. Only the Holy Spirit can give you joy.

I declare: "How I see my future begins with how I see myself."

MARCH 22

Start praying for strength. Venting will not help; it only brings on symptoms. I have learned the hard way not to vent to others. I started a journal instead. Tell God. Or write it down and throw it away. Good idea to just keep it to yourself. Privacy is power. Your love life and your income should stay private. Wake up early. Work harder today than you did yesterday. Read positive faith-filled books daily. Never go more than three days without exercise. Eat right. Do not listen to gossip. Develop a beautiful attitude about life, the best advice. Save money weekly. Most importantly, listen to the Word of God.

Choose your friends to match your goals. Be independent. Read, read, read. Look after your health. Love yourself first. When life is sweet, stay thankful; if not, work on being more grateful. You are here to work on yourself and to help encourage others. We must help others, but we must not do for them what they will not do for themselves. God will work with you.

I declare: "My feet will never take me where my mind has never been."

MARCH 23

Your brain will do everything you tell it. You can retrain your brain daily. Feed it faith. Feed it truth. Feed it love. Feed it with positive daily words from the Word. The Word is so powerful you will feel amazing. One of the best things you can do for yourself is learn to master the art of changing your thinking. When you stay focused on the good, even the good gets better. It is time to get happy. Staying stuck in negativity, with sadness, anger, and overthinking, is not working. Call me crazy, but I crave and love to see others happy and successful. Focus today on rebuilding yourself, and the right people will find you. Everything begins and ends in your brain. You cannot control one thing, but you are thinking anyways. The most useful asset you have is the beautiful positive picture you can hold in your mind about living a positive, powerful life. Whatever you hold in your mind is exactly what you will live. Success comes from what you do consistently. Seek God first, read daily devotionals, listen to all positive talks, and declare: "I can, and I will." Always forgive; this is how you heal from the inside out. Train your mind to see the good in everything.

I declare: "I am in the process of becoming the very best version of myself."

MARCH 24

How easy it is to forget to appreciate things. Take time out to sit back and learn to be thankful for the simple things and times in life. Look across the table and look at the person's face you are talking to. Never stop trying. All the best love stories have one thing in common; you must go against all the odds to get there. Do not tell yourself you cannot. With or without someone by your side, you must achieve the goals that you have set. Sometimes, God does close doors, but we must move forward. Trust the transition. The truth about a relationship is two imperfect people refusing to give up on one another. You are not perfect. Forgive yourself. Practice self-care. Be crazy enough to believe God can do anything. There is something good in every day.

I declare: "I will guard my heart, for everything I do flows from it."

MARCH 25

Secret wrongdoings can steal your joy. Do not let that happen. There is beauty in childlike faith. And you are worth it. Find the positive in that negative situation. We must work on forgiveness and forgetting. Do not compare yourself to anyone else; that is an insult to you. I have no room for negativity, and neither should you. There are hidden blessings in every struggle. The mind is so powerful. We can create or destroy. You can only change yourself and others by your example, not your opinion. Just because you are struggling does not mean you are not blessed. You will succeed because you keep going and going and going. Hard work always pays off. When I feel tired, I start to think about how great I am going to feel once I finally meet my God-given goal. That is so worth it all! Be picky this day: with your friends, your time, your thoughts, your words, and your clothes. That thinking will determine the quality of your whole life. Believe in you. God doesn't create junk.

I declare: "I will not dwell on what I don't have at the expense of what I can have."

MARCH 26

Be teachable. Focus on people who inspire you. *Life* is all about how you handle plan B. It is not how big the house is; it is how happy the home is. The most beautiful thing for me to say is, "I have fallen apart, and with God, I have survived." I traveled through madness to find myself, and the Lord strengthened every weak area of my life! Take the first step. Some do not know the new me; I put back my pieces differently. Glory to God. You are going to be happy, says life, but first, the world will try to make you strong. But remember, your strength only comes from God and His Word. There is power in the Word of God. It is life-changing. Someone said, "I do not know how you do it." I said, "I was not given a choice." But I choose to follow God, His Word, and start a relationship with Him. My whole life changed for the better. People say a lot. So, I watch what they do. Every next level of living will demand a different you. Grow in God's grace and love. Get spiritually mature.

I declare: "I am teachable, God is showing me what to do daily, and I am an honor student of His."

MARCH 27

Chase purpose; do not fear failure. Somewhere someone is looking for exactly what you can share about your life growth. A key to success is to start before you are ready. Things that try to pull you down to drown you have taught you to swim. Life is trying to teach you something. Be positive. Never think you are above or below anyone. Keep a humble spirit. My future is in God's hands. God called me out of darkness into His marvelous light. One day, I decided I was over feeling like I was downtrodden, and I haven't looked back since. I was radically saved by God. I wanted to change my life. I smiled, and I knew it was time to move on. Life went on, only better. What an amazing thing that the darkness of this world can serve to push us into the character and goodness that God predestined us to become. I must praise His name! I pray, I work, and I have faith. I do not beg, force, or chase. Mighty women of God do not have attitudes; we have standards. A stronger woman stands up for everyone. It is not your job to like me; it is mine.

I declare: "I release unhealthy thoughts and emotions. Unfruitful relationships must flee my life. Negative words I have spoken over myself, I let them go. I will live in peace, freedom, and joy. I forgive others so I can move on. For I am a chosen person."

MARCH 28

And there you are, moving on despite how difficult it has been. You must remember to be thankful for the trouble you do not have. If you are not smiling, you should because the Lord will never leave or forsake you. When God is silent, He's doing something for you. Laugh when you can; it is a cheap medicine. It's not your fault how you were raised, but it is your responsibility to grow in Christ. Make that decision and work on yourself. Someone needs to hear your story to get set free. He who the Son sets free is free indeed. If the Lord asks you to do something for His ministry, do it scared. The Holy Spirit is the One who will work through you. Trust Him to show up. Meditate in the Word of God, for it fills you with boldness and success. Keep calm and carry on. Everything you need is in the Word of God. Do not be deceived; you must stay out of darkness. Stay in God's marvelous light.

I declare boldly Psalm 1:1–3 over your life; insert your name in it. There is power when you claim the Word of God over yourself. Life-changing.

MARCH 29

We all face trials in life. What does God want us to learn during them? Through the storms of devastation, God promises to make something good out of it. Romans 8:28—declare it. When troubles flood over you, consider it an opportunity to count it as joy. If you look to the world, you will be depressed. Be still. Do not be afraid. Just believe the Word of God. You will receive power when the Holy Spirit comes upon you. Ask. God's angels are watching over you (Psalm 91:10–11). Faith moves mountains. The most important thing you can do when praying for something major is to believe. Do not become weary; it is a trick of the devil. God will provide. Let everything you say be good and helpful. When I am afraid, I put my trust in Him. Do not let your heart be troubled. Trust Him.

I declare: "I will just trust God and let go of fear, worry, and doubt and live in total peace."

MARCH 30

Those who trust in the Lord will find new strength.

Nothing can stop God's plan for your life. The Lord is greater than the giants you are facing. Do not worry; instead, pray. God can restore what is broken and change it into something amazing. Faith is what you stand on. I thank God for protection from what I thought I needed. If you are praying about it, God is working on it. Hallelujah. He is preparing you now for it. "Lord, change me from the inside out."

I declare: "I am surrounded by God's favor."

MARCH 31

Zipper up! It is amazing how fast you will forget your problems if you simply stop thinking about them. Do something uncomfortable today; zip it. Stop talking about your problems. Your words affect your thinking. If you stop talking, you will stop thinking about it. Try it. Think out of the box today. It is not the future; you keep repeating the past with your words. To change, you need to be sick and tired of being sick and tired. If you are reading this, I challenge you to dedicate the next six weeks exclusively to watching your words. No fallback. No negativity. No past rehearsals. Just concentrate on your new goals, your positive faith-filled readings, your positive faith-filled YouTubes, your health, and seeking God first thing in your day. Do the work. Do not be distracted by things that have nothing to do with accomplishing your goals. Sometimes, there is no support system; it is just you and your grind. I want to be a better person all the way around. It is time for new beginnings. I am invested. I am made from faith, prayer, self-love, and affirmations. You can't break a person like that. Pity party canceled.

I declare: "I will keep the zipper on today, no matter how badly I want to interject my opinion or thoughts."

April

Understand [this], my beloved brethren. Let every man be quick to hear [a ready listener], slow to speak, slow to take offense and to get angry.

James 1:19 (AMPC)

Your words are powerful. Be careful what you speak.

APRIL 1

Breathe. Everything will be fine. Even if you are praying the same prayer a million times, know this, your prayers never fall on deaf ears. He is our God throughout our lifetime until our hair is white. He made you, and He will care for you. He is going to carry you, do not panic. God will answer you when you least expect it. God's plans will always be better and more powerful than all those disappointments you are having right now. God is faithful. I will walk by faith when I cannot see. Do you trust God when His answer is, "Wait"? If it was not for that struggle, you would not have that strength! God is building you right now, not breaking you! Dear God, help me break away from the things that are breaking me. Nothing will hold you back more than your own insecurities. Wake up to your calling! Ask God to balance you. I admit it, I cannot do anything without Him.

I declare: "Show me Your ways, Lord; teach me Your paths."

APRIL 2

Your prayers are more powerful than education, finances, or a degree. When I wake up in the morning, I seriously do not want to do any part of my goal list. I *push* myself and end up having the most amazing, powerful day ever. *Push* yourself. Pray until something happens. Life just does not happen. You make it happen by your daily habits and choices. Please let me encourage you to jump up, feet hit the floor, and start speaking out loud what you will accomplish today. Be so beautiful that others crave what you have. And that, my dear, is discipline. Two pains: Pain of regret or pain of discipline. You must fight through some bad days to earn the best days of your life. Teach others what you know and do. Create the life you cannot wait to wake up to. Be tougher than your life is. Note to self: You are not too old, and it is not too late. Oh, and always be kind! Miserable and negative cannot stay!

I declare: "First thing: this is the day the Lord has made that I will rejoice and be glad."

APRIL 3

Death and life are in the power of your tongue. Speak life! Your entire life can change in one year, but first, you must love yourself enough to realize you deserve more. Stop thinking you have no purpose. Stop living in the past. Declare, "My future is in God's hands." Drama will not follow you if you mind your own business. The same people who can be candy to our eyes can also be poison to our hearts. Study their ingredients. If you are together, you are a team. What makes a team is respect. We respect because we trust and truly care for one another. Do not allow others to make more withdrawals than deposits. Loving yourself is not vanity; it is sanity. I love and adore positive people. Words are free. It is how you use them that may cost you. Pray that God will use you to change lives. Make this day count. Cancel the pity party. Four important words to live by are love, honesty, truth, and respect. Without them, you have nothing. Self-care tip: Be careful what you say about yourself and others; your brain is listening. Some people do not need advice; they need deliverance. I know God is working, so I smile.

I declare: "My future is in God's hands."

APRIL 4

I believe there are no random meetings in our lives. Brief encounters can open good doors. You are growing into a new you. For everyone who asks—receives, he who seeks—finds, and to the one who knocks—doors open. Because greater is He who is in you than he who is in the world. Draw near to God and stay there. If you seek Him early and diligently, you will set your day up for success. Be not hasty in your spirit, for anger resides in the hearts of fools. And that could be you or me without Him. The same power that raised Christ from the dead is living in you. For one thing I do know, I was blind, but now I see. The goal in life is not just for self, selfishness, or greed. I am fighting to be a better me so I may encourage and encounter others to be a better them. Wake up! Commit to this every day. There is no shortcut to being a better version of yourself. Pay attention to those opened doors. Your example is not the main thing in influencing others; it is the *only thing!*

I declare: "I have been crucified with Christ, and I no longer live, but Christ lives in me."

APRIL 5

Do not let what you see happening allow you to forget the promises of God. If it is not your circus, stop attending. My favorite line is, "Not my monkeys and not my circus." Minding my own business has given me so much freedom, and it is free. Today is a brand-new day. Do not just step into your comfort zone. Get going with the plan the Lord has given you from His Word. Comparison is the biggest thief. You are enough, and you are more than a conqueror. Declare: I am expecting something wonderful and new today, for I am fearfully and wonderfully made. I was designed with a great purpose. My childhood and past will not dictate who I am. My new choices and goals are me. I have responsibility to make my life incredible. I am a doer of the Word. I will live life with great intentions and on purpose. I am directed by the power of the Holy Spirit. I am victorious over all my situations.

I declare: "I praise You because I am fearfully and wonderfully made; Your works are wonderful. I know that full well."

APRIL 6

The worst kind of pain is the pain you receive from the one you explained your pain to. And that is where you can receive your biggest growth. Nothing can go against the plan of God. So be careful how you respond with your words and actions. This is so important for your next move. Encourage yourself to stay joyful and hopeful as you put your trust in God. God will do exceedingly and abundantly more than you could ever ask for. You need to stay hopeful and not let your own words sabotage your God-given dream.

I declare: "All things work together for the good of those who put their trust in Him."

APRIL 7

Like you, I am still working on myself. I am seeking God first so I can walk in joy and happiness. Ask yourself today, "What can I do to walk in happiness?" Do not ever quit working on yourself. We never stop growing, and we always need to do the hard work! The day you or I think we have reached where we want to be is the day we stopped learning. Wherever you live, whoever you are, and whatever you do in life, the Lord has given you creativity to put that work in motion so you can glorify Him. You have resurrection power to be creative. Be creative today. The Holy Spirit lives in you. Let us refuse the ideas that do not work and pray for the new ones that will work. He has given us freedom.

I declare: "I have been faithful with a few things; I will be putting You in charge of many things."

APRIL 8

Your words establish faith! Refuse to let hard things knock you down. Fix it? Force it? Figure it out? Frenzy? Do not think you can fix anything. That will not work. "*Faith* it" is a skill that needs to be learned. Successful people embrace uncertainty. Prayer and gratitude will set the day and the pace. Do not go into battle without it. No complaints. No doubt. No hopelessness. You are not alone. God is right there with you. Quitting is not an option. Focus on faith and give it over to God. Laughter is the new medicine. Write down all the things that are going great for you, and keep reading them over. That will boost your gratitude meter. What is meant for evil, God can turn into good. Know God's love. No *fear*. Trust God: you cannot fix one thing! Standing *firm* on the promises of God! Stay focused on *faith*! Confessing the Word over every situation is why it is so important to pray.

I declare: "I will stand firm, and I will win in life."

APRIL 9

Stop making excuses because you love them. What you tolerate, you will live. One-sided relationships are those that do not value you or respect you. Red flags are deal breakers. Red flags are issues for a toxic relationship. Invite God into your relationship or dating process. No one wants to be with someone who will not show others they are a couple. We end up toxic because we do not stand up for what we believe in. We let them slide because we fear. Develop healthy barriers today for how you are going to be treated in all areas. You are responsible for your relationship, nobody else. If you do not want it done to you, do not do it to others. Do not play the victim when you helped create the circumstances of the circus. Recognize when someone makes you question if you are worthy of being loved as a red flag. Without pure trust, you will not and cannot have a happy, strong relationship. All we have is now. Become a doer of God's Word.

I declare: "I trust in and rely confidently on the Lord with all my heart and do not rely on my own insight or understanding."

APRIL 10

It takes two to tango! Stop kidding yourself, good or bad. If your relationship is amazing, congratulate both partners.

Things do not just happen; you made it happen intentionally. Are you suffering in your relationship? Remember, it takes both partners to get it back on the right road intentionally. It takes hard work, disciplined habits, powerful words, and seeking the Lord together as one flesh to have an amazing marriage. It is amazing how others crave what you have but do not put the effort and energy seeking the Lord for it! God is not a respecter of people. He will do what He has done for us, but you must be willing to do the heavy lifting and the unpacking of bad baggage together as one flesh. If God is for us, who can be against us? Declare: Blessed, fortunate, and favored by God are the man and woman who do not walk in the counsel of the wicked or the ungodly. Nor stand in the way of the scoffers. But their delight is in the Lord. They will be like trees firmly planted by the water, which yield fruit in due season. Their leaf will not wither. And whatever they do will prosper and mature. I prayed this over our marriage for forty years. I am a tree firmly planted; I will prosper and come to maturity. No weapon!

I declare: "I am blessed, fortunate, favored by God, and I do not walk in the counsel of the wicked or ungodly."

APRIL 11

Sometimes, my greatest accomplishment is keeping my mouth shut. Sometimes, the best part of my job is that my chair swivels. Sometimes, it may look like I am doing nothing, but in my head, I am so busy. Some days, it is hard to find motivation. Some days, motivation finds you! I am, like you, currently under construction. Wake up and work hard at your goals, do not let life knock you out with "*sometimes*"! Do not trust your tears; they do not give you strength. We cannot choose the music life plays for us, but it is our responsibility how we dance to it. Not anyone else. You must have the passion and strength to believe that you can overcome anything. Push yourself because no one else is going to do this life for you. There is something beautiful to prove to yourself just how strong you are in the Lord. Dance before the Lord with all your might. Sometimes, you must turn your thoughts off and stand firmly on the promises of God. God's got this in His Word.

I declare: "I press on toward the goal to win the (heavenly) prize of the upward call of God in Christ Jesus."

APRIL 12

No matter how strong you are in the Lord, the devil will take advantage of your mind to stay unfocused on what is important. Warning warriors: We must act by stopping our mind when it wanders and discipline it to stay focused on the promises of God. It is not easy to discipline your mind when you are in the fire. The devil wants to make you think that you cannot be helped, healed, or encouraged. But when you get God involved and come against His action for your mind, the devil is defeated, and you are on your way to winning another battle of the mind. Stay focused and start right now to prep your mind for action. Holy Spirit, I know firsthand how fast the devil can fool me and take over my thinking. I stand in awe of Your power, and I thank You in advance for giving me the mind of Christ and helping me overcome a wandering mind. It stops right here, right now. I declare and decide today no weapon formed against me shall prosper. I am winning the battles in my mind starting today. Your plans for me are for progress and victory. And I ask it all in Jesus' name.

I declare: "A happy heart is good medicine, and a joyful mind causes healing."

APRIL 13

It is a beautiful thing to stand on the Word and say, "I fell apart, but I declared the Word of God daily, and I survived supernaturally." It does not make sense, but it is not supposed to. It is called faith. Declare: I will rise. I will always rise. Do not doubt that, even for a second. If you are pretty or handsome, you are pretty, and you are handsome. But the only way to be gorgeous and beautiful is to be loving and understanding. Otherwise, it is just congratulations about your face. Be careful who you vent to. Stop trying to skip the struggle, which is how you mature spiritually.

Beauty will always attract the eye, but it is your attitude that captures the heart. You can tell a lot about a person by what he chooses to see in you. The more you work on yourself and become better, the better person you will attract. Your life is someone's dream. Do not live ungrateful. The real mark of your maturity is the ability to stay humble and kind when others are not. That is your real power. You do not need to wrestle someone about something to prove that you are smart. Wisdom comes from God. You seriously do not have to prove anything. If you are giving your all and it is not enough, you may be giving to the wrong person. Stay in prayer. Ask God to show you the truth about things. He is the only way!

I declare: "I will rise; I will 'always' rise!"

APRIL 14

The kind of person you are is recognized by the friends you pick. Misery loves company, so stay clear of the negative ones. God takes care of people through other people. Your greatest friendship desire should be with God. The more you read the Word of God, the more disciplined you will be. You can tell a tree by the fruit it bears. Bad company can and will corrupt good character. There are people that can drain you and pull your energy down by gossip. Be aware. Pray for them and shorten your time with them. They are just like the flu, contagious. Be selective about who you hang with. Settle for only the best without judgment. You pick what you reap. Words are powerful; be sure what you want you speak over yourself, your family, and others. He gives grace to the humble.

I declare: "A good tree cannot bear bad fruit, nor can a bad tree bear good fruit."

APRIL 15

Gradual growth is God's process. First, you must forgive yourself. Then declare I am not what happened to me as a child or my circumstances. I am a product of my choices and my decisions. You must remain strong when you are feeling weak. Stay low-key; everyone does not need to know everything about your past. Your heart just needs time. When the time is right, the Lord will let you use your past for someone else's growth. For with God, nothing is impossible. Be careful with your words, for they have power. Just remember, even your worst day only has twenty-four hours. Stay strong in the Lord. Life is only as good as your mindset. Negative minds kill the ability to do what is good and right. Intention is everything. Humble yourself under the mighty hand of God. Everything I *am* I owe to God; everything I have come from God; to Him be the glory. Do not let anyone who delights in false ways disqualify you. Keep quiet about your merits; then you will have good success. Speak kindly always. The devil is the fault finder.

I declare: "I am not what happened to me as a child or my circumstances."

APRIL 16

May I repeat this: Nothing changes unless you make the change. This moment right here, I know you want to quit, but this is the moment you need to *push* yourself hard.

The enemy will seek to confuse you with wrong thoughts. Protect your thoughts by reading the Word of God. Declare: To-day, I can change my story. Boss up and change your life. Your entire life can change in a year. What would you do if you did not have that fear? If you believe you can do better, then do better. We cannot become what we want to be by remaining what we are. The key is to never stop doing right. Your life cannot get better by chance; it gets better by changing your habits. Pray, patience, positivity, and peace. Declare: I believe in myself. I am whole. I am kind. I accept myself. I accept change. He is risen. There would be no Christmas if there were no Easter. And He died for us all!

I declare: "I have the ability to change my story. Boss up and change your life!"

APRIL 17

Important message: Do not give advice unless you are asked for it. Stop focusing on what others should be doing and focus on you. Get yourself off the hook. Stop and breathe. God is up to something greater than we imagined or thought possible. Fast from hurting words. Fast from anger. Fast from selfishness. Fast from grudges. Pray as if every week was Holy Week. Have an attitude of gratitude. Love is patient. Love is kind. It does not envy. It does not boast. It is not proud. Although Easter time spells out beautiful, the beauty of new life can be each day. What do you need to change in your life? Cry out to the Lord and ask the Holy Spirit to fill you up with what you need. Grace will flow down so we may become like Him. When He was on the cross, guess what? You were on His mind.

I declare: "I am fasting from negative words, hurtful words, anger, and selfishness."

APRIL 18

Renew. Rethink. Reflect. Repent. Rejoice. It is finished.

Declare: And by His stripes, I am healed. Trusting God with everything. Be that encourager today. What the Lord has done for me, I cannot tell it all. God has not given you the spirit of fear. You must not get tired of doing good, for you will reap at the proper time if you do not give up. Nails did not hold Jesus to the cross. Love did. Thoughts for Holy Week. This is the week that changed the whole world forever. Forget the past; look forward to what is ahead. The greatest gift that Easter season offers is hope. Hope to love again. Hope to live again. Hope to laugh again. This is a privileged time to draw near to Him. Resurrection, not just in books but in everything that blooms in springtime. Bloom where you are planted!

I declare: "No weapon formed against me shall prosper, for by His stripes, I am healed! In Jesus' name. Amen."

APRIL 19

Overthinking again? Tell that negative thought that meets inside your head to sit down and flee. True love is not found; it is built. In springtime, may your faith in God bring peace to you and your heart. No pain, no palms, no thorns, no throne, no gall, no glory, no cross, no crown. Joy is what happens when we allow ourselves to recognize how good things really are. Your life is made up of mistakes and learning, waiting, growing, practicing patience, and being persistent. Smile; it is a new day. Two thousand years ago, Jesus ended the debate on which lives matter. He died for all!

I declare: "For God so loved the world that He gave His only begotten son..." (John 3:16a, NKJV)

APRIL 20

It is all about the one in your life who helps you calm the storm. Who is it for you? Be thankful for that special one in your life! Stay thankful for the one who makes your bad days better. And with the one that says, "My life has changed since I met you." Appreciate those that free their time to be with you or those who talk to you in their free time. Learn the difference. A relationship is to make each other better. Build up one another. Be the peace to one another, not the problem. Which one are you? Supporting one another is free. It is a choice. Selfishness will not work; unforgiveness will not work. If they act like they can live without you, let them. Intention is everything. The ones that pray together stay together. Do not let others influence your emotions. Be with someone who invests in you. The man needs to believe she is a gift; a woman needs to believe he is a gift as well. Teach our sons to be that kind of man. Teach our daughters to treat him as a gift too.

I declare: "I desire and delight in (steadfast) loyalty rather than sacrifice and in knowledge of God more than burnt offerings."

APRIL 21

Stay determined! Doubt your doubt before you start doubting your faith. Everything has a beauty to it. The problem is, not everyone sees it. The time to be amazing is right now! Make your sacrifices. Do not say something unless you mean it. Amazing people do not just happen. I am intentionally speaking what I want to be over myself daily from His Word, and that is working for me. *Stop* underestimating yourself. You can do that, and you will live a beautiful life too! What makes you different makes you beautiful! Let that faith be bigger than your fears. Be uncommon. Do not stay stuck in those bad habits! How is it working for you? Today is the day our lives changed forever on being a new creature in Christ. He did it for you!

I declare: "I remember (with awe and gratitude) the wonderful things that He has done, His amazing deeds."

APRIL 22

There are simple truths to speak out loud when you are in a spiritual battle. It is finished. God's got this. The Lord will fight for me. Fear must bow; it has no grip on me. I am a mighty man/woman of God. I am a new creature in Christ. I am fearfully and wonderfully made. "Not today, devil." Do not speak poorly. Love and do good. Faith will cast out fear, while fear will always cast out your faith. I need to depend on the power of God. Man without God can do nothing. Start your day with simple yet powerful prayers: "Guide me, protect me, bless me, and forgive me, Lord. And I give You all the praise for the brand-new day." Pray for open doors in your life today.

I declare: "Hear now my words: If there is a prophet among you, I, the Lord, will make Myself known to him in a vision, and I will speak to him in a dream" (Numbers 12:6, NKJV; paraphrased).

APRIL 23

Know how to take authority over the test you are in with the Word of God. Get into agreement with what God is saying. It is just a season. You must go to battle. Fight the good fight of faith. Break those generational curses over your life. Breathe. God's got you covered. Do not fear; you have too much to do for Jesus. The enemy knows if you read your Bible, you will break off generational curses. Keep your thoughts clear of fear. It is a process, and everyone's test is different. God answers prayers, so I say, "Thank You, Lord." He has been so good to me, but I have had to go to war! You do not have to face this test alone. You have the same power inside of you that raised Lazarus from the dead. It is inside of you! Get ready for that breakthrough. Speak life!

I declare: "I will guard my mouth (thinking before I speak) to protect my life. The one who opens his lips wide (and chatters without thinking) comes to ruin."

APRIL 24

Know the mighty supernatural power within you. If some-one has wronged you, they will need more of your prayers. And if they are enemies, we are ordered from the Word to pray for them with forgiveness. Evil is the abuse of free will. Do not waste time trying to figure out if you love your neighbor; we are instructed to act as if we do. We are what we believe we are. We all think forgiveness is a great idea until we must forgive some-one. I give in, and it truly works. Try it. For ourselves, we accept excuses so easily; for others, we do not accept them enough. He is working all things out! Yes, I will choose to praise Him. I will glorify His name. His love endures forever. Yes, I will! Guard your heart. Pray for God's wisdom. Avoid complaining, gossiping, and being negative. We cannot become like that, so it is important to guard our minds too. He certainly answers. Doubt your doubt.

I declare: "Be kind and helpful to one another, tenderhearted, for-giving one another (readily and freely), just as God in Christ also for-gave you."

APRIL 25

Lay it all down; God's got this. God got this. You must go through the process of spiritual growth for maturity! You must guard your heart and thoughts and stay in forgiveness! It is a must! We must walk in spiritual wisdom and maturity! Yes, spiritual maturity! You must lay down fear and doubt to crucify the flesh. It cannot go where you are going, and you cannot go where God is going to take you with self-seeking. Declare: I am walking into my divine purpose intentionally with the power of Jesus Christ. I am healed and set free. The past is not your future. You must trust God for your future. It is called tough love over yourself! The past is gone. If you dwell in the past, it creates sadness, frustration, bitterness, hatred, and envy, which kills brain cells. Scientists have proven it creates diseases. Be thankful for the scars: without them, you would not know God's beautiful heart. I stand in confidence that God's got this. I am thankful for the scars. Absolutely the truth! God is for us. He says we are loved. He says we are strong. He says we belong, and we are His. So, I believe it. He is my identity. I am set free. Trust in God breeds joy. Doubt is distress.

I declare: "I am walking into my divine purpose intentionally with the power of Jesus Christ."

APRIL 26

Your past cannot be changed. Never regret a day in your life. Never reply when you are angry. Do not wait for things to get better. Be happy right now and be that blessing to someone in your life. Welcome to adulthood. Never doubt what one prayer can do. Keep praying; God is hearing you. Prayer is the cure for the confused mind, a broken heart, and a weary soul. When we pray for each other, something supernatural takes place. Hallelujah. Take a moment right now and pray for the person on your heart! God can restore. Do not try to make people change. Pray, let God do it. The poorest person on Earth is not without money but is the one without Jesus.

I declare: "I will pray and go into my most private room, close the door, and pray to my Father who is in secret, and my Father who sees (what is done) in secret will reward me."

APRIL 27

Despite what the enemy does, trying to seduce them, warrior is that spiritually strong person who wakes up or destroys them. A warrior is the person who will declare the victory before they even see it. A warrior is the person who believes by faith they will receive their miracles because they know the mighty God they serve is alive inside of them, and they know their God will never leave or forsake them. They know the Lord will fulfill His promises. Pull back your hair, set your sights on God, and declare to finish the race that is set before you. You are a warrior. Declare: I am a mighty warrior. I am more than a conqueror. I am a blood-bought child of God, and I will see victory. Do not worry about people who wrong you. God sees it all. God is with you, and that shall sustain you.

I declare victory before I see it manifest in the natural.

APRIL 28

Jesus is my *Rock*, and that is how I roll! Faith in God includes the faith in His plan and timing. God has never failed me. Look forward with lots of hope. Never look backwards with that regret. There is no fear here. Stop wishing. Start worshiping. I am moved by what I believe, and I believe God. I am not moved by what I see. The Lord will change your life. He will transform your life from sickness, disease, fear, doubt, loss, and lack. Take your authority over the devil. No fear. God is in control; relax. Overthinking leads to negative thoughts. Holy Spirit, You are welcome here. Nothing is too big for our God.

I declare: "Now faith is the assurance of things hoped for and the evidence of things not seen."

APRIL 29

Do not let that devil fool you. He is under your feet. Protect your mind! Stay in the Word. Praise is your answer to that dilemma. Stay strong in your praise. Mental stability is required. Your mind can be renewed daily by you starting your day seeking the Lord. Prepare your mind for this battle. How do you fight your battles? With praise and prayer? Stay right there. Your weapons of warfare are in the Word of God in Ephesians chapter 6. Stay mighty in the Word. And keep that flesh weak. Emotions will lead you to defeat every single time. We are Spirit people led by the Holy Spirit if we ask Him to. Get ready; your breakthrough is right around that corner. Stay prepared. Get into the Word of God and let it get into you. Stay in the Word and protect your thinking! It is a ticket to success! Use failure as a stepping-stone to your next level; it is a way up! Your Bible is not for information; it is for your transformation.

I declare: "My mind of the flesh is death (both now and forever because it pursues sin), but the mind of the Spirit is life and peace."

APRIL 30

Are you discouraged? The remedy is the Word of God to feed your mind and heart for new strength. Never let a test stop or intimidate you. Right now, right here, let it push you to a higher level of motivation. Pray more than ever. Trust more than you have before. Walk around expecting the impossible situation to turn possible. Nothing is impossible for our God. Be bold in your prayer life and stay persistent. Keep on asking; you will receive what you have asked for. I want to ask, seek, and knock because I believe with God, everything is possible. Do not open your mouth if you would be ashamed of your words later. Whosoever keeps his mouth and his tongue keeps his soul from great trouble. There is so much Kingdom work to be done. Get ready; God is not finished with you yet! Get excited.

I declare: "On the day I called, You answered me; You made me bold and confident with (renewed) strength in my life."

May

And whatever you do, whether in word or deed, do it all in the name of the Lord Jesus, giving thanks to God the Father through him.

Colossians 3:17 (NIV)

Your words are powerful. Be careful what you speak.

MAY 1

The most courageous decision that you can make each day is to be in a great mood. You have to get to a point in life where your mood does not shift based on insignificant actions of someone else. You can remain humble and know that you bring good things to the table. God knows when it is time to be seen. Be patient. People may throw stones at you. But do not throw them back. Collect them and build an empire. Instead of getting defensive, just say, "Thank you for letting me know." Talk to God before you start overthinking again. For He who is mighty has done great things for me (Luke 1:49). Love (1 John 4:18). Work the Word, not your personal agenda. Run to the Father. A bad attitude is like a flat tire. You cannot go anywhere in life until you change it. Before you say anything, think how you would feel if someone said it to you. Fairness counts.

I declare: "Through God, I will strive to change my attitude for the better so I can be happy regardless of the circumstances."

MAY 2

Do not wait until this battle is done. Declare your victory now, and thank the Lord in advance. Be still and know that I am God! The Lord will fight for you. A mind controlled by the Holy Spirit is life and peace. Quieting yourself may be a huge challenge. And making your mind come under control may feel impossible. The struggle for control is normal to you. Pray for a Holy Spirit intervention and ask Him to control your thought, life, and mind. This will help smooth out the rough areas of your personality. You must set aside time daily to seek, pray, ask, and rest in the presence of the Holy Spirit. He will fight for you. God is a God of complete order. You do not have because you do not ask (James 4:2). The Lord is my portion; therefore, I only hope in Him. I surrender my being into His hands to mold and shape me to be like Him. The flesh has no Holy Spirit's power. None!

I declare: "With God we will gain the victory, and he will trample down our enemies" (Psalm 60:12, NIV).

MAY 3

Look for the gold in others, not the dirt. Everything changes except God. Act in God's Word; do not react to your situation. Try to smooth out the situation by managing your emotions. Thoughts determine behavior. There is one thing you can always count on in life: change. People change, circumstances change, our bodies change, our hair color changes, and even the size of our clothes changes. If we let change in life upset us, we will always be in a state of panic and fear. So, we need to get our thoughts and emotions in order, according to the Word of God. Filling your mouth with the Word of God will be your mighty weapon of warfare against any situation. By confessing the Word by faith, your voice activates your thought life for the best. God's Word is forever. Your and my heart will overflow with a good theme, and we will do awesome things. Adapt to change by writing God's Word on your heart first thing daily. Get quiet before the Lord. Be loud and expressive in your praise only. It aids in defeating the devil. It is the only way!

I declare: "The Lord is good to those who wait (confidently) for Him, to those who seek Him (on the authority of God's word)."

MAY 4

Only God knows what you have been through. His Word is the spirit of life. If you are not at peace, then something else has taken place in your life, and it is not from the Word of God. His promise for you and me is to give us abundant life and peace through His Holy Spirit. Examine yourself, then encourage yourself. We are transformed and purified by the renewing of our minds. God wants us to live peacefully with all men. If we are not living in the spirit of peace, there is something wrong. If you are uneasy about not being peaceful, you are in a good spot. Wherever I go, I want to be salt and light with a peaceful attitude for the glory of the Lord. He wants us to be peace to all men. Most important of all, God is with us. Do not lose your peace today. And if you do, repent and get back on the peace track.

I declare: "I am continually renewed in the spirit of my mind (having a fresh, untarnished mental and spiritual attitude) and put on the new self (the regenerated and renewed nature), created in God's image."

M A Y 5

Constant complaining only magnifies your problems. Stop complaining. If you want to stay stuck, continue to complain and let those negative emotions drain you. We must train our minds to stay in a positive mode. If you stay focused on all the things that are going bad, you will continue with the doom and gloom. May I suggest something that will get you out of the negative into the positive? Make a list of all the beautiful things that are going right. This alone will help you to stay positive and build up your faith. You must learn to *speak* positively. Choose your words wisely. You must decree and declare positive affirmations over yourself so you can live it. This should become your new language. It is called the language of *success*. Practice makes positivity perfect. Pray about training your mind for success. It is all about your own personal daily routine.

I declare: "The words of a wise man's mouth are gracious and win him favor, but the lips of a fool consume him."

MAY 6

Fix your eyes not on what is seen but on what is unseen.

What is unseen is God's presence. Get excited again. Do not let your doubt make you doubt what God has told you. Let God deal with people. You are only supposed to be salt and light, not the judge or the critic. Your time and your energy are extremely valuable and priceless. It is not your job to fix or change people. Remember, you will become ten times more attractive not by your looks but by your acts of kindness, love, respect, honesty, and the loyalty you show to all people. Advice: Never criticize or ridicule others that choose differently than you. You and I deserve to be around people who treat us like we matter every day, not just when it is convenient for them. You are priceless. You are valuable. But you will receive power when the Holy Spirit comes on you. Ask daily to be filled with the Holy Spirit. Speak: "Lord, Your servant is listening!"

I declare: "My eyes look directly ahead and gaze in front of me."

MAY 7

Be set free. It all starts in your mind! It is okay to have an opinion, but an opinion is only important to the one that thinks it. If it is not from the Word of God, it is not for you. He is perfect in all His ways. That includes His Word. When I think of all He has made, no praise is great enough to express how great He is. Are you fearful, depressed, angry, feeling lonely, or worried? Remember, we serve a *mighty* God who created the Earth by His spoken Word. So, whose words are you listening to? He made the sun, the moon, and the stars. And He made you! Take a moment to read the Word and listen to faith-filled messages to get back up and serve. Fear must flee, self-hatred must bow down, and sickness and disease must go. "Lord, You are Mighty. In Jesus' name! You are amazing."

You can do all things through Christ. If your thinking is stinking, so is your life. Only you can change you. I am blessed and highly favored by God. I will live my destiny. Do not listen to naysayers or dream killers. You are covered by the blood of Jesus.

I declare: "Lord, You are mighty! Your name is excellent over all the earth."

MAY 8

You are Jehovah-Jireh and Jehovah-Rapha. He is your provider and your healer. Through this trial, the Lord will show you a new life. He will do something amazing for you. Listen for His voice to guide you. Trust Him, and you will be strengthened by Him more than you could ever imagine. He loves you just as you are. Love from Him is unconditional. Nothing will separate you from the love of God. You were handmade by Him. Share your heart and mind with Him.

"Set a guard over my mouth, Lord. Let my mouth stay shut when I am tempted to say anything that is not from You."

You never know how strong you can be until being strong is the only choice you have. Pray with fierce boldness. He has commanded you; be strong and courageous, do not be terrified, do not be discouraged, for the Lord your God will be with you wherever you go!

I declare: "Do not speak in the ears of a fool, for he will despise the (godly) wisdom of your words."

MAY 9

We need to learn how to be "now" people and focus on what God is doing right now. Are you wasting your energies trying to fix things that you just cannot fix? Try sowing seeds from the Word. If you talk most of the time about what is going wrong, about what you do not have, about how bad you feel, well, that is what you will have more of. If you make that hard decision right now to talk about the goodness of God and what He can do, you will feel more powerful and positive. Declare: I am sowing seeds of faith that will produce positive results. Our words will produce a negative day or a positive one. Declare: I put my trust in God to do what I cannot do. And all that worrying is for nothing. I am blessed. I am healed. I am delivered. I am protected. I am directed by the power of the Holy Spirit. I have wisdom from God. I am planting seeds of faith with my words to produce a harvest of peace. He is your only source.

I declare: "I am sowing seeds of faith that will produce positive results."

MAY 10

You will look back and be amazed. Nothing is impossible with God. Won't He do it like He said He would? But you must put action to your faith by always trusting Him. One thing to always remember: *Do not* major in minor things! It is not a goal of an extraordinary person. Prophesy: He is leaning in my direction. This is my season for grace and favor. This is my season to reap what I have sown! I have got a seed in the ground! I do not care what your circumstance looks like. He will always do it. There is a breakthrough in heaven with your name on it! There is a miracle with your name on it! Send a praise up! We are in a battle, but God will always give the victory if we fight with powerful prayer!

I declare: "Without faith, it is impossible to (walk with God and) please Him, for whoever comes (near) to God must (necessarily) believe that God exists and that He rewards those who (earnestly and diligently) seek Him."

MAY 11

Your victory loss will begin in your mind. The spiritual battle will begin by building up your faith level. If you are hesitant, get in the presence of God and ask Him to meet you where you are at! Think of all He has already done that will cancel your weariness. Do not let your own heart and mind condemn you. Understand your mind is imperfect. God is greater than our thoughts and our hearts. And He knows all things. *Hope!* With man, this is impossible, but with God, all things are possible. He is the Creator of the universe. And He chooses to make His home in our hearts. Your choices matter. There is no condemnation for those who belong to Him. No pain, no gain. The reward of blessings always goes through a series of testing with obedience. Stay faithful in the little things; this is how you grow up spiritually.

I declare: "Even before there is a word on my tongue (still unspoken), Lord, You know it all!"

MAY 12

There is an amazing power in forgiveness. Practice being a good forgiver. That is how you win the war. Our struggle is not against flesh and blood but against the spiritual forces of evil. Do not be fooled. Defeat the enemy by staying in forgiveness. Forgive anyone who offends you. The Lord forgave you! Be aware, and do not allow the bitterness of forgiveness to hinder you. It will damage your health, it will drown your peace, it will poison your mind, and it will stop your joy. We do not have the right to judge. The Bible calls that "not wise." "Lord, teach me to do Your will." Remind yourself the gift of salvation is yours. We must work on our growth daily. Do not be conformed to this world but stay transferred by the renewing of your mind! The mind is powerful!

I declare: "I am kind and helpful to one another, tenderhearted (compassionate, understanding), forgiving one another (readily and freely), just as God in Christ also forgave you."

MAY 13

Be careful not to be suspicious of others; this is how the devil gains a stronghold in your mind. It is all about trusting others. What is real love? Read 1 Corinthians 13:1–13 until it gets into your heart, mind, and soul. If we are not careful about our emotions, we can poison our own minds against others. Suspicion can destroy a business, a church, a family, and your own home. It will lead you down a dark, lonely road. The reading will help you form a kind of love that is so important for your Christian growth. Declare: "I thank You, Lord, for helping me overcome any kind of suspicion. Fill me with Your agape love."

We are better to trust others and find out we may be wrong about them than to live a life of distrust. It is a distraction from the enemy to keep you stuck in deadly emotions. Forgetting is a choice like forgiveness. Fill your mind with valuable things. Forgive and forget. Get your eyes off others and focus on the Lord!

I declare: "I will focus on the Lord and overcome any suspicion I have."

MAY 14

Be careful not to let anything take the place of the Lord in your life. If you struggle with thoughts of fear, worry, doubt, jealousy, anger, or bitterness, it may be that you have invited a person or a vision, such as an idol, to get in the way of your faith. Get in prayer and ask God to reveal what is going on in your heart today! Seek God first and pray for a new thirst and hunger for Him. Then let go of what He reveals to you. The lack of peace will be your key to know something is not right. God is a God of order. His desire is to bless you so you can be a beautiful blessing to others. Do not keep struggling with those things that stop your growth and poison your peace. Seek ye first the Kingdom of God and His righteousness. When you do seek Him first, His blessings will overtake you. Be patient. God is not done yet.

I declare:

> *Peace I leave with you; My [perfect] peace I give to you. Do not let your heart be troubled, nor let it be afraid. [Let My perfect peace calm you in every circumstance and give you courage and strength for every challenge.]*
>
> *John 14:27 (NKJV; paraphrased)*

MAY 15

Whatever God calls you to do, He equips you to do it well! Take time to plug into the Word, open your Bible, and listen to the download God has just for you. Work on you, for you. Talk to God before you overthink. Never think you are above or below others. Keep a humble spirit. Today, think about all that you are instead of all that you are not. Courage over fear. Pray big even when you feel small. Some of the best days of your life have not happened yet. Chin up; you are not struggling. You are more than a conqueror. "Heavenly Father, strengthen those who may be growing weary. Show them that the best things in life are the people they love. Help them to believe in miracles, wait for Your answers, and trust Your timing."

Mornings are better when you talk to God first. You have been assigned to this mountain to show others that it can be removed. Trust God. Because of your faith, it will happen.

I declare: "Trust in and rely confidently on the Lord with all your heart, and do not rely on your own insight or understanding."

MAY 16

Do not get stuck in how you feel! The devil wants you to pay attention to your feelings. Jesus wants you to pay attention to His truth. Maybe today you just need to declare out loud: I forgive me! I believe God. Do you believe? I believe in what He has promised me. "I trust You, Lord." Declare: I believe God. He will do it. Never give up. But you must remember: Do onto others as you would like them to do for you. This is a *powerful*, simple best practice. You cannot think just about your own household. You must move beyond. Walk with integrity. Life point: Do not judge. Pointing fingers creates war. Stay helpful. Stay faithful. Your blessing is on the way. No one wants to be around people who just tolerate them. Live with acceptance. Make others feel important just like you do your own family. Pray for them. Make it your best practice to encourage everyone you see today, no matter what. Be a hope dealer. What you plant, you will pick. Forgiveness starts with you.

I declare: "Therefore, encourage and comfort one another and build up one another, just as you are doing."

MAY 17

Declare: I am the healed of the Lord, *no* weapon formed against me shall prosper in Jesus' name. If you are feeling unimportant or insecure, remember you belong to the King of kings, the Lord of lords, and the God of gods. God is about to change your story. What you think you have lost, He is about to restore. You and I are not called to shine our own light; it is not right. You and I are called to reflect His light. Your own prayer life is that bridge between panic and peace. Stop underestimating what God is doing in that season of waiting. Worry is not a bridge. It is handled by God. You must begin to believe. Focus on God. You have 99,000 blessings. God is the forgiver, the Savior, and the healer. No failure, no sin, no brokenness; you are His child. You are covered by His grace. His story. His glory. Chill. God's got this.

I declare: "I am healed of the Lord, no weapon formed against me shall prosper in Jesus' name. Amen!"

MAY 18

Are you going to fall for that lie and trick again? Feelings!

I feel, I feel, I feel. *Stop!* Change is the only power that truly works, as in changing the way you think. If you do not decide to change that mind, your life will never get better. You can go to sleep holding your Bible, and that will not change you. You can go to church every Sunday, and that will not change you until you listen and change your thinking. You can change where you live, and that will not change you. You must stop your feelings of emotions and think about the promises of God over those problems that are trying to overtake your thinking. You may be saved, but you will not live the abundant life if you allow defeating and hopeless thoughts to rule your thinking. Attitude is everything. Change your thinking for success. "Deliver *me* from old thinking patterns. I receive it. I am directed by the Holy Spirit."

I declare: "I will not live by my feelings; I will live by the Holy Spirit guiding and directing me and die to my flesh."

MAY 19

We are reminded in 1 Thessalonians 4:11 to mind our own business. It is an interesting instruction. We need to refrain from opinions of others that do not concern us. We are instructed to live peacefully, and we are to tend to our own business and stay out of other people's affairs. And we are to be dependent on no one and in need of nothing to be self-supporting. We are to make it our ambition to love and encourage others. We are urged to excel and practice this more and more. Some of us are naturally gifted as encouragers who make everyone around us feel amazing. We may not be born with that gift. We are not to be faultfinders or critical beings. This truth will set you free. We are to be this publicly and privately. Pray your way through this day. Your challenge is to go out this day and encourage that person that stands in your way. Be that kind of encourager.

I declare: "I will make it my ambition to live quietly and peacefully and to mind my own affairs and work with my hands, just as I have been directed so that I will behave properly."

MAY 20

All that matters is that we pray the way the Holy Spirit leads us and that we are connected with true faith and make our request known to only Him. The Word is a weapon. It is your weapon to attack your doubt, worry, and fear. Do not worry about tomorrow, for tomorrow will worry about itself. Each day has enough trouble of its own. I must stand on the Word of God! I know I cannot do *one* day without reading His divine Word. That is the only way I attack doubt, worry, and fear. It is my weapon. I must renew my battlefield mind daily. I must speak the Word. I must declare the promises of God over myself, my day, and my family. To me, it is a must. No question at all. The Word of God is my weapon. I am a believer. I have a changed heart. I have new behavior. I have results because I speak God's Word. One of the most powerful ways against the enemy is to know the Word of God and *speak* it out loud against the lies of the enemy; talk back to that liar with the Word. I know I am more than a conqueror, and so are *you*!

I declare: "God did not give us a spirit of timidity or cowardice or fear, but (He has given us a spirit) of power and of love and of sound judgment and personal discipline (abilities that result in a calm, well-balanced mind, and self-control)."

MAY 21

Any kind of negativity is very unattractive to God.

Boasting and gossip are behaviors we should avoid too. You will not be known by your credentials but by the power of your genuine love. That grateful heart you have is a huge magnet for miracles. Edit your own life ruthlessly. After all, it is your masterpiece that you will give to God. Do not save your beautiful self for special occasions! Live you to the fullest. Always ask yourself, "Is what I am doing supporting the goals that I am trying to create?" Visualize your higher nature, which is the nature of God, and start showing up as that. Daily reminders: I am amazing; I can do all things through Christ. Positivity is a choice; I am valuable, and I am prepared to succeed. You owe it to yourself to become everything you have dreamed of being. God created you. You are allowed to grow and change. Being happy never goes out of style. God's favor and blessings on my life are lightening this load and taking the pressure off. I am loved, called, and chosen. Do it now.

I declare: "I will be happy and do good."

MAY 22

Gratefulness does not come naturally, but grumbling does. I challenge myself daily to stay disciplined. It is a choice I must make too! Self-control is resisting the temptation to speak negatively during that difficult situation. Your mouth and mine want to blab out what we feel during that time. To stop it before we say it takes self-control. We lose the battle by murmuring and complaining before we think about what we are going to say. This is self-pity and fear, and it will not defeat the enemy of our soul. We must stay connected to the Vine. God has a beautiful plan for us to thrive, and it is not called fear, worry, or doubt. We will wither and die like a broken-off branch from a living tree when we do not stay connected to Him. We can work ourselves up to a frenzy of fear fast. The key is to ask God first, then receive it by faith, and lastly, stay thankful. "Thank You, Lord, for all Your goodness to me. I know I cannot do this life without being connected to You first."

Stay connected; there is power in the name of Jesus. Ask, receive, rejoice.

I declare: "I will keep the unity of the Spirit through the bond of peace."

MAY 23

It is up to you to break generational curses. When they say, "It runs in the family," you say, "This is where it runs out." Encourage yourself and move on. The worst enemy is self-doubt. Talk to God before you overthink. Do not just listen to what others say; watch what they do. Repeat after me, "It is not my responsibility to heal, save, punish, or control others; that is God's job." You are only called to be salt and light. Break the patterns of behavior that stop your growth. Change the behavior to get that beautiful result. You are not stuck. *Fear* is a liar. God is awesome. Stay in prayer. Your answer is closer than you think. Declare: I cancel and destroy every attack of the enemy over me and my household, in Jesus' name. It is not about you; it is all about what we do with our lives for Him.

I declare: "I cancel and destroy every attack of the enemy over me and my household in Jesus' name."

MAY 24

Look for a partner that prays for you and with you. One who will point you to God when you feel disappointed. One who will treat and speak to you as if you are the finest person in the world. You are a team. You are going to dream the rest of your life together. Each husband should love his wife as much as he loves himself, and each wife should respect her husband. Therefore, what God has joined together, let no man separate. Declare: My partner believes in me and supports me fully. A real man chooses to honor, love, respect, adore, and be faithful. Be the woman who makes the bad days better. The woman who makes you say, "My life has changed since I met her." Guard your thoughts and your words. A husband and wife can love each other best when they love God first. Love is praying for each other. There is no such thing as "happily married forever." You must work at it... intentionally!

I declare: "Let us love one another, for love comes from God. Every-one who loves has been born of God and knows God."

MAY 25

Flow with the spirit of God. Invite the Holy Spirit to fill you up. It does not matter what you have done. The grass is not greener on the other side. It is fake. Your battle is my battle; we must fight together. True love is never found. It is built. Pray for grace. My goal is to be a better version of myself. I want to carry the glory of God. I need a relationship with the Holy Spirit. We all need to flow on the glory. I believe in the supernatural. We are called to make God's presence known, no matter where we come from. Pray to learn the Kingdom principles. Do you want a supernatural flow of the Holy Spirit to see miracles? This is a journey. Ask the Lord to heal your heart against the spirit of heaviness. Daily ask the Holy Spirit to guide your whole day. It is amazing what He will do just for you. God wants to use you. You create your life. Ask so you can become and work out your miracle-working destiny.

I declare: "I want a supernatural flow of the Holy Spirit to see miracles."

MAY 26

You were not called to fix others, only to love them. Faith in God does not have an expiration date. A day without faith... just kidding. I have no idea what that is like. You are who you listen to. Headphones on! World off. What are you listening to today? Listening daily to faith-filled messages is life-changing. Faith building is my therapy. Ah! Faith. When the faith is good, life is always so much better. Faith has the power to make us joyful. It inspires us to praise the Master of the universe, our mighty God. The secret to a happy, power-filled life is to listen to more faith-filled messages and take less advice. The Holy Spirit will show you what to listen to. Just ask! Lost in faith. Find your freedom in God. Listening to faith-filled messages daily can improve memory, strengthen your immune system, and reduce depression. Where others' words fail, *faith* speaks. Do not stop the faith. Never stop learning or listening to the Word. Life without faith, I can't.

I declare: "For it is by grace you have been saved, through faith— and this is not from yourselves, it is the gift of God."

MAY 27

Your mind is like your home; you must clean it up every day and be careful who you invite in. Some people will never like you because your Holy Spirit irritates their demons. Our tongue holds blessings and curses, so let's watch our words. A silly woman looks at what a man drives. A queen looks at what drives a man to be her king. Are you hoping for that dream car, or dream house, hmmm... or maybe that special someone? When the whole time, the blessing is that you woke up this morning. Let us celebrate that daily. God is my strength. Train your mind to hear what God whispers and not what the enemy is shouting. Be like a diamond, precious and rare. I am impressed by the way someone treats others. Give the gift of your absence to those who do not appreciate your presence. Know your worth. Just because you are a soldier does not mean you should let others put you through war. Most important in life—God. Greatest weapon—prayer. When others do you wrong, forgive quickly and watch God do you right. Do not fear.

I declare: "The voice of the Lord is powerful and majestic."

MAY 28

Misunderstood? Being both soft and strong is a beautiful combination only a few have mastered. Pray for inner strength. I know mountaintop experiences feel amazing. I also know rock bottom teaches you lessons that mountain tops never will. As you are shifting, begin to understand the value of your voice and that some situations no longer deserve your time. You are not stuck. Avoid people who act like the victim when confronted with their toxic ways. Be mindful what you put into your thinking emotionally; that is part of your daily diet too. Get excited again. Cut out all negativities. Say goodbye to people who just do not care. Pray to win with action, not words. Start calling yourself healed, happy, whole, blessed, and prosperous. No negative words, please. Ask the Holy Spirit to live in you. The Bible not once says, "Worry about it." But it clearly says, "*Trust God.*"

I declare: "Those who hope in the Lord will renew their strength. They will soar on wings like eagles; they will run and not grow weary; they will walk and not be faint."

MAY 29

Still grumbling? Humbly come before God and surrender your heart. Stop letting deadly emotions be your decision-maker. Stop, pray, and let the Holy Spirit guide you. When I am worried, it is usually because I am trying to do everything, and then I remember that God handles it all. That is when I regain my peace. Bless those who curse you, pray for them. It is going to be okay. Never pay back evil with more evil. Show everyone that you are honorable. Do everything you can possibly do to live at peace with everyone. They say a fool vents his anger to all. Be careful how you live. Let God handle your enemies. Treat others who make mistakes the way you need God to deal with you when you make a mistake. Do not let darkness exist in the natural to replace the *divine* supernatural.

I declare: "Blessed are those who act justly, who always do what is right."

MAY 30

If it costs you your peace, it is way too expensive. The heart may be deceived. The Holy Spirit not only shows you what is true but guides you into the full truth. Do not follow your emotions. Follow the conviction of the Holy Spirit. I took my troubles to the Lord; I cried out to Him, and He answered my prayer. Now, I am walking in *victory*. Do not worry. He sees, He hears, and will deliver. Do not be afraid. Fear not. Our God does not give a spirit of fear. You did not create yourself. Your human reaction is fear. Do not allow it to cripple you. Put one foot in front of the other. The enemy knows fear will cripple you. Live fearlessly. Your decision. Are you going to entertain fear today? Exchange the fear for an opportunity to pray. I want everything God has for me. The other side of fear is the blessing. Stand firm. *Stand.* Do not lean to your own understanding. Sitting is passive. Require yourself to stand. Stand firmly on what God says. Believe.

I declare: "I stand firm, and I will win in life."

M A Y   3 1

What do you need? Compassion? Understanding? Love? Kindness? Acceptance? Patience? If you need any of these, sow them towards the people around you, and you will receive a double portion back. Do not be deceived; whatsoever you sow, you will reap. If you sow to the flesh always, you will reap disappointment, discouragement, and destruction. Declare: Lord makes me aware of sowing to the Holy Spirit so I will reap life and have it more abundantly. Whatever you need today, *sow that!* Be intentional and stay interested in helping to change lives for the better. Live your best self today.

Double *blessing*.

I declare: "Peacemakers who sow in peace reap a harvest of righteousness."

June

Do everything without grumbling or arguing.

Philippians 2:14 (NIV)

Your words are powerful. Be careful what you speak.

JUNE 1

Stay kind. It makes you stand out in a crowd no matter where you are or what you are doing. God's Word is powerful. You must be obedient to it; it will not cover up ugly actions. There is power in persistent prayer (Micah 7:7). Believe in what you pray for. Being different is a good thing. It means you are trusting the Holy Spirit enough to be your true self. If life does not challenge you, it will not change you. Being a beautiful or handsome person is an attitude. You know you are on the right healthy path of life when you become uninterested in looking back at the past and getting stuck in the old way of thinking. Do not stay mad. Do not get even. Rise above even being right. Life is short. Declare: I am not going to put you down, even if you are tearing me apart and bad-mouthing me. I realize you are already down. Here is my rescue story; I will be the best version of myself to you. With love. The first thing you should understand about me is that I am not you. I will be the person who breaks the cycle for the glory of God. I have a purpose, and I am on a mission for God. I will not respond to rudeness, jealousy, or unkindness. Do not waste time on revenge. There is no market for your emotions. Never advertise your feelings; just show your beautiful attitude. Celebrate others' success, no matter what.

I declare: "I am a child of God."

JUNE 2

The truth hurts, but it will free you. If you are tired of being the same, it is time for you to get out of the way. Shame, rejection, self-hatred, addiction, abortion, and negativity are huge traps to *stop* the flow of the Holy Spirit. Are you tired of it yet? Let God show you what to do. It is too easy to compare and constantly complain. That must go. Do you want to be happy? Only you can change you. Why stay stuck? There is something so incredible just for you, ordained by God, if you will bow down and release any of the above and just forgive yourself. It is that easy. And then stop talking about the situation. You are set free. Believe He who the Son sets free, and He will, is completely free indeed (John 8:36). You only must believe it and receive it by faith. Start setting new goals, read faith-filled books, and listen to faith-filled sermons. Everyone can find the time to do this. This is so powerful that the enemy makes you think this is too simple and, of course, that you do not have the time. What does a liar do best? Lie. This is your sign to start today to change your destiny! You still have six months left to this year. You can do all things through Christ, who strengthens and prays for you (Philippians 4:13). It is not easy, but you cannot live happily without it!

I declare: "I am free from all guilt and condemnation."

JUNE 3

Patience is learned! There are things you will never under-stand, and that is okay. The flesh desire must be dead. You must fulfill the true desire of the Holy Spirit and stay pliable in the hands of God. Works of the flesh must bow down. He is work-ing! Faith cannot be seen at all. One thing I know for sure is your faith can be felt, not seen. The Bible says true faith always produces good works and healing words. Think about that. We are displayed by the fruit we carry. We do not cause problems. God's Word says we will be known by our heartfelt fruit: meek-ness, humbleness, love, kindness, gentleness, and patience. And for us to display our fruits to others. Faith without our work is just dead (James 2:26). I believe others can see and feel what we believe. True faith always produces great works. We are justified by God by our faith alone. We are justified by peo-ple by our works of action of our faith. Our *fruit*. What kind of fruit does your life display all day? Be a fruit inspector over your own life! Are you joyful and fun to be around? Look at the fruit of your own walk!

I declare: "But if we hope for what we do not see, we wait eagerly for it with patience and composure."

JUNE 4

You must be a doer of the Word, not just a hearer (James 1:22). Using discernment when tempted to give our opinion that is not asked for is so powerful. You believe your words are powerful, right? But saying the right thing at the right time needs prayer. Sometimes, things unsaid are a best practice. Take your time today to listen to others who are different than you. They may be in your life for a very good reason. Show acceptance. Be respectful. Your way is not the only way! Be sensitive to others' needs. Do not be a bully. People will not want to be around people they do not trust. Be a strong encourager. The world has enough judges and critics. Sometimes, keeping your opinion to yourself, especially if it is a negative criticism, is a powerful move. Do not damage close relationships. They may be the ones to help you in your future. Be the pat on the back. Take a little extra time today and a little more effort to be that extraordinary person. Successful people are more than conquerors. No matter what! Worship God. Our worship is our devotion to God; it shows our intimacy to Him.

I declare: "I will keep my opinion to myself; it's only my opinion."

JUNE 5

The greatest test is how you handle people who mishandled you. Only you can leave an important imprint on people that no one else can. God created us with a fingerprint that no one else has. Think about that! This day is going to be a "God made a way" kind of day. When you are feeling disappointed, He will strengthen you with joy. Remember, your daily habits decide your future, not you alone. Your seeds matter. No seeds, no harvest. *Speak life* over yourself and everyone around you. You just cannot change the past; stop thinking about it. Be a prayer warrior; your prayers can move mountains. This is just a chapter, not your whole life story. This shall pass. Master this day. Then just keep doing that every day with your new daily habits. Passion for God is the most attractive feature you can possess. Ask God to show you how to love like He does. Imagine "that someone" who talks to God about you. To solve that problem, stop participating in the problem. It is that simple. In other words, stop talking about it.

I declare: "I am growing and becoming strong in spirit, filled with wisdom; and the grace (favor and spiritual blessing) of God is upon me" (Luke 2:40, NKJV; paraphrased).

JUNE 6

Do not worry if others do not like you; most of them do not even like themselves. A thankful heart is a receiving heart. Ask God for wisdom. Do not get frustrated today because you are on a training ground. Seek Him wholeheartedly. He brings you to a point where you must only rely on God. Keep loving Him. You are just being stretched. Ask and believe. He knows the plans He has just for you. They are plans to prosper you, not to prison you. Plans to give you hope, not hopelessness! Plans to give you an absolutely abundant future. This is your encouragement today. Do not be vulnerable to your own defeating thoughts. You must live in the very present moment. The secret thing in life is to belong to God. "Rejoice in the Lord, you righteous ones; Praise is becoming and appropriate for those who are upright" (Psalm 33:1, AMPC).

I declare: "He knows my plans for my future."

Stay right there.

JUNE 7

Remember, you are not a helpless victim! You have authority, as a powerful child of God, to be a mighty warrior. The blood of Jesus drives the enemy away always. This is a powerful weapon of warfare. Be aggressive in your prayer life. Take authority over your day first thing in the morning. It is your responsibility to keep evil in its place. As a believer, you have this amazing authority. Have confidence when you pray. Obedience is extremely important, seeing your prayers answered. Check your heart out? Is it right standing with God? Pray boldly today. Receive by faith. If your answer seems to be stopped or delayed, trust His timing. His ways are higher than our ways. Do not lean towards your fears. God in you is greater than that! No fear in God's love. God is working in you. Do not lose what you have already gained.

I declare: "Keep your [my] tongue from evil, and your [my] lips from speaking deceit" (Psalm 34:13, NKJV).

JUNE 8

Are you desperate for ease? The best thing I ever did was put all my *faith* in God. From another point of view, praying the Word of God over my giant prayer seemed so much more possible. Look out for your tongue; it is in a wet place and may slip. Influence the energy around you with amazing grace. Begin to live as though your prayers were already answered. He's got you like He always has. You may be struggling, but you keep declaring, "I am blessed. I am favored. I am loved." You cannot manipulate the outcome. Do not overthink. Be strong. You never know who you are inspiring. Thankful. Grateful. Faithful. Journey. Prayer is the cure for a confused mind, a weary soul, and a broken heart. Keep praying. Pay attention to the scriptures that keep showing up. He wants to speak to you.

I declare: "I am blessed, I am favored, I am loved."

JUNE 9

We need to humble ourselves. Our great attitude is our best asset! Attitude is our winning edge. It will make you successful. You cannot buy your attitude, but you can make a choice to live with an amazing one. No one knows what lies before us. If you have a positive attitude, you can run things smoothly. Live today with your best attitude forward. I humble myself with an attitude of repentance and humility in the presence of the Lord. He will order my steps. He will lift me up and give me my purpose. We can plan, but it is up to God to direct our path. Plans for tomorrow. I will submit and resist being in control. Praying over my thoughts and words. God has given us power over the choice of our words. You cannot bless and curse with the same tongue. Choose blessings overall. It is so worth it! I bless you in Jesus' name! No weapon. He is my Deliverer.

I declare:

> *Humble yourselves [feeling very insignificant] in the presence of the Lord, and He will exalt you. [He will lift me up and make my life significant.]*
>
> *James 4:10 (AMPC)*

JUNE 10

Every one of us is very important. And each of us can become a person who desires to encourage others daily. You do not even have to have it altogether yourself. The only thing you truly need is a heart that seriously cares for others. Realize this! Life is not a dress rehearsal. Do not wait until tomorrow to start. Start right now with the people that are the closest to you. If you have a kind word, share it now. Whenever a person is around you, take that opportunity to *lift* him or her up! You know there is a difference in hurting and helping others. Do unto others as you would want them to do unto you. It is that simple. We must be consistent in making others feel valuable. It is the little things we do and say daily that make a positive or negative impact on our relationship building. Today is that special day to put this into a best practice for the rest of your life. I love being intentional and interested in making others feel very special about themselves. Be that positive influence wherever you go today. You've got this! This will help build all your relationships. Remember, "if" is not a dress rehearsal!

I declare: "I am overcome with joy because of God's unfailing love."

JUNE 11

Do not neglect to pray for strength and pray against the tricks of the enemy daily. The Holy Spirit Himself will empower you, giving you inner strength. This is what will keep you going. Apart from Him, we can do nothing. Do what you can and leave the rest up to Him. Stop worrying about tomorrow! Your future is secure in Him. Look to Him daily, and you will be filled with radiant power. The Lord is Holy, All-Powerful, Pure Love, Mighty with grace, Everlasting Joy, the Healer, your Provider, Forgiver, and your Prince of Peace. Take hold of these facts today and believe everything you need is right inside of you. Your human nature is what will stop you. God can do all things. Be made new. God's got this. Stop trying to figure out what is happening. Rest in Him. Pray continually. Let the Holy Spirit take charge of this day and every day. Ask Him to take control of your mind! You are a new creature in Christ.

I declare: "I always pray; I don't faint, quit, or give up."

JUNE 12

Fact: The right person makes your life soar. They do not change you; you change yourself because you feel free to be who you were created to be from their unconditional love. Everyone is born creative. What do you plan to do with the rest of your life? For what this is worth, it is never too late to be what you want to be! Pray for strength to do it. Talk about what you love. When you feel free enough to be loved, you grow into who God created you to be! Creativity is who you become. Let us do this! If you cannot say something nice, speak in tongues. Words are powerful; they will stop your creative flow if they are negative. Very little is needed to make your life joyful. Always be you. People that matter do not mind, and the ones that mind do not matter. What you give to one person overflows into the lives of all the people that person impacts. Knowing what others need is the key. Everyone needs encouragement, help, and friendship. There is no such thing as a self-made man or woman.

I declare: "God meets all my needs according to His riches in glory by Christ Jesus (Philippians 4:19–20)."

JUNE 13

Remaking your life can only be done with the power of the Holy Spirit. There is never a day that I will not or do not think of you. Grief, I have learned, is only a strong love. One thing I realize is that grieving is a part of life. This is a price you pay for caring for the people you have lost in your life and loved. You will celebrate and live many good days, and you will have, suddenly, trips of grief come over you unexpectedly at times. It is a sort of sadness laced with healing that you will carry for the rest of *your* life.

Because death has stopped the plans, cut off your relationships, and forced you to learn to live without the ones you love, you will change for sure, but for the better. It is a sensitive bruise that does not go away. But now you have awareness and deep compassion for those who are grieving. Grief to everyone is difficult, and it has no expiration date. Grief makes you a better, loving, and more compassionate person. Become the things you love the most about the ones you have lost. Hold on tight to the love, not the loss. Sometimes, those memories and beautiful moments sneak out of my eyes, and yes, they roll down my face. No one ever explained that grief can feel like fear. I have been changed forever. But I am stronger, wiser, and better. What happens is you miss the future. Stay strong. Do what is right for your soul. Keep Him close.

I declare: "I am rooted, established, strong, immovable, and determined (1 Peter 5:9–11)."

JUNE 14

Walk like it! Talk like it! Dress like it! And wait for that godly person who treats you like you are a child of the King. Practice self-control. Be hospitable. Live with modesty and loyalty. Use wisdom laced with kindness always. Stay teachable; you just cannot know everything. Hardworking with sacrifice looks good on you. Staying honest in sticky situations keeps you trustworthy. Stay directed by the Word and not the world. You can be a gorgeous spirit, charming and irresistible for the rest of your life, if you nail down that selfish desire. It has to go. There is nothing more classy or powerful than showing forgiveness laced with grace to others who do not deserve it. Respect yourself. Anyone can hold a grudge. Give it all to God, and go relax.

I declare: "By my steadfastness and patient endurance, I shall win the true life of my soul (Luke 21:19)."

JUNE 15

I have learned to shake off rejection and move on. In my younger years, I felt rejected about everything in my life. And then I found out that trusting God over all my insecurities by reading the Word transformed my whole thinking. Whew! Then I learned about the fruit of the flesh and the fruit of the Holy Spirit. Galatians 5:22, plant this in your heart for it is life-changing. It is a physical manifestation that will happen after we believe the Word of God. In this world, we are taught to believe what we see. In God's Kingdom, we must believe first, then in due season, we change for the better by the power of the Holy Spirit. What a true blessing by faith. Ask God to help you see what you need to work on. Find your true purpose in life. The devil knows your weakness...mine was a spirit of rejection. It has got to go!

I declare: "God, all things are possible with You!" (Mark 10:27)

JUNE 16

One of my best practices is knowing when it is better to remain silent and not reply, knowing it will start a war. Just let the Lord fight this battle. Silence is golden. And the Bible says, "[...] never answer a fool" (Proverbs 26:4a, NKJV; paraphrased). It is seriously none of your business what others say about you. And minding my own business most times has been a huge blessing to me. I enjoy keeping my opinion to myself. And remember, most people only think *their* opinions are sacred. Do not waste your time. Live your purpose. And just stay out of others' business. This is called anti-stress. Why get involved when it is not your circumstance or circus? Best thing I have ever taught myself is to mind my own business. God will fight your battles if you take your hands off it. Relax. Deep breaths. God's got this. It is none of your business what anyone thinks or says about you. God thinks you are amazing. He just loves you because He created you just as you are. He died just for your salvation; that is what He thinks of you! The Holy Spirit is your Comforter; call on Him. Be sure your heart is pure. He will fight your battles.

I declare: "I am living the life of the Spirit because the Holy Spirit dwells within me (directs and controls me) (Romans 8:9)."

JUNE 17

Stop listening to the noise of this world! What do you ben-efit if you gain the whole world but lose your own soul? Accept yourself and move on. No need to defend or explain. Just seek how to restore your soul. Take care of yourself and learn to love who God created you to be. Nothing can separate you from the love of God. The Lord is close to the brokenhearted (Psalm 34:18). He has heard your prayers and seen your tears. He will help you. He is sending you the Holy Spirit. Ask. When He hits your life, you will see a change. Depression must lift, illness must flee, so strongholds and curses will be broken. The Holy Spirit will bring you peace and understanding with direction. Leap! It is a new season of joy for you. God is your comforter. We love because He has loved us first (1 John 4:19). "Lord, I open my being and turn my heart towards You. Fill me." Do not pan-ic. He will help you.

I declare: "I will live a balanced life because God's Word states that if we are not well-balanced, we open a door for Satan to come in and devour us."

JUNE 18

This life right now in front of you is far more important than the life behind you. Today is a gift. All we have is now. Put your phone down. Hate no one, no matter what has happened. Stay humble, no matter how successful you become. Stay positive, no matter what test you are in. Be generous, even if you have been given little. Forgive all, especially yourself. Always pray for the *best* for everyone. God will never put weight on your shoulders that you are not meant to carry. Strong? No, I am far from it. What you are seeing is simply a weak me with a very strong God. Read your Bible. You are who God says you are. This difficult road is leading you to a beautiful destination. You must be at your strongest, especially when you are feeling your weakest.

I declare: "The eternal God is my refuge and dwelling place, and underneath are the everlasting arms (Deuteronomy 33:27)."

JUNE 19

Ladies, do not call a man or chase him down. Let him make all the efforts to get a hold of you. He should do the calling or texting. You are a prized possession, a gift made by God. The Bible says the man should pray and look for his wife. It never said the wife should look for her husband. Never sacrifice your relationship with God for a relationship with another person. God will not bless a relationship He is not involved in. Your relationship must draw you closer to Christ. Get close to God first. Men of God Care for her like *Boaz*. The wrong love makes you wonder where God is. The right love makes you feel His presence everywhere. Let God do the heart-changing. Be with someone who wants to love God with you. Your true peace comes from knowing that God is in *control*. Let God write your love story. Dance with God, and He will let the perfect man for you cut in. I know this source of knowledge because it was my experience. You can never build a "Kingdom" with someone who craves attention from the village. Sometimes, your Knight in shining armor saves you from a fool.

I declare: "[...] as for me and my house, we will serve the LORD" (*Joshua 24:15b, NIV*).

JUNE 20

Do not give the devil a foothold. If anger is in your heart, it is a strong foothold for the devil (Ephesians 4:27). Do not worry about what others say to or about you. God will never discourage you, ever. If others do, it is not from God. It is not from the Holy Spirit. And Jesus would never hold you down when you are broken. I know, I have been there! God will not put you down; He will lift you up. A true follower makes beautiful possibilities for others. Walk away from those who point out your mistakes. Walk away from arguing; it accomplishes nothing. Walk away from trying to please people; it is a losing battle. Walk away from the self-righteous; they know only themselves. Walk away from things that poison your Holy Spirit. You are beautiful. The older I get, I know the importance of walking away from situations. Stay kind, value yourself, and know by walking away, you value your self-worth. Never forget how far you have come. Be an awesome, amazing encourager. We are human, not flawless. Our greatest role in any relationship is to be a light, not a judge. Open your eyes. You love not by finding the right person. The true love of God is learning to see an imperfect person *perfectly*. If someone treats you badly, there is something wrong with them, *not you*.

I declare: "I choose to walk away from negativity. I choose to stay kind and value myself."

JUNE 21

A toxic person does not break your heart; they break your spirit, which is why it takes so long to heal. The enemy will only bother you when you are trying to live a holy life. God is building you. God can make that mountain of fear bow down. Prayer is your passport to Holy Spirit's power. Pray. Wait. Trust. Believe in what you pray for. Declare: I am prepared to succeed. I am enough. Love is chasing me down. I am walking in God's unconditional love. Ask yourself, "What am I doing? Does this support the life I am praying for?" Talk about all your blessings. Not your problems. If you want to soar, get rid of everything that weighs you down. Stop being a prisoner to the things you just cannot change. You cannot blame a clown for acting like a clown. Stop going to the circus. I was accustomed to complaining and venting. Then I started praying. I realized I did not need sympathy; I needed strength. Until God opens that next door, praise Him in the hallway.

I declare: "I am prepared to succeed; I am enough; love is chasing me down."

JUNE 22

Do you believe you are forgiven? Dare to begin to believe, this day, how much God truly loves you! Your past is under the blood. You are already complete in Him. Failure is a step to success. Do not get stuck in the failure process. Remember that your spiritual being is far more important than any material thing you may have. Do not let your possessions destroy you. The Lord is your security, not what you own. Do not boast. Do not let your past chain you to your future. You have been set free. With God, nothing is impossible (Luke 1:37). It is important to renew our mind first thing daily. Do not get stuck in that "me, mine, and I" attitude. It is not about you or what you did or can do. It is about living your purpose for the glory of God. You were created to *do* something for the Lord, and it is to help others, not for self-promotion. It is for His glory. Get into intimate security with God; it is far more valuable than all your possessions. Long-term trials are very draining. The Lord is your shield and strength (Psalm 28:7). He is your protection. Read the Word daily. He is the Alpha and the Omega. Rejoice in the Lord always. I know it can be difficult. Do not get panicked. Manage your emotions. It is important. Be intentional about spending daily time with just you and God. You cannot leave home without it. Choose by faith to walk in the power of the Word!

I declare: "I am made whole through the power of Jesus."

JUNE 23

Is human rejection God's divine protection? Although rejected, do not operate out of a spirit of rejection. Handling rejection teaches one to wait patiently. The Lord does not reject. He does not abandon. Do not be upset when others reject you. Nice things are rejected all the time by people who do not recognize value. Rejection merely alerts you that others have failed to notice what you have done or what you have to offer. Jesus was rejected by men but chosen by God (1 Peter 2:4). Declare: I am anointed. You are not less valuable after a rejection. Rejection is a huge sign to redirect your gifts elsewhere. Remember this, a crystal-clear rejection is always better than a fake promise. I felt my rejection was clearly God's protection over me. It is hurtful to feel unwanted. People will show you how they feel. Pay attention. The most powerful motivation is rejection. Trust God that there is a better yes down the road. See rejection as redirection to something much better. There is redemption too. Pray for that over yourself. Understand that others' judgment of you reflects their insecurities, hurts, or what they thought their life would be. Rejection can't stop the plan of God. Rejection is something or someone that God wants out of our future. Rejection does not stop you; it will stop life. Never give up.

I declare: "I will use rejection as a strong stepping stone for great success ordained by God."

JUNE 24

Think about making every day a *masterpiece* of life!

No, this will not be easy, and yes, this will change your life forever. Of course, it is hard; it is supposed to be. If it were easy, everybody would be doing things the same way. But life is different and difficult for everyone. May the next few months be a season of magnificent transformation. The two things you can control are your attitude and your effort. Tell your mind to get out of the way. Right now, become the best version of you. Do it for you. Declare: I am physically strong and mentally indestructible. I am directed by the Holy Spirit. I believe in the person I want to become. Some of the best moments in life are not when everything is going right. It is when your plans are falling apart, and you keep pushing yourself forward. Always keep the Holy Spirit fire alive. Life will always have ups and downs. Be miserable or motivate yourself. It is always a choice.

Push yourself because no one else is going to do this for you. This is about being consistent for your lifetime. Live your masterpiece daily.

I declare: "I am physically strong and mentally indestructible."

JUNE 25

Discipline is not enjoyable while it is happening. Self-discipline will not just happen. It is a daily practice over your faith, mind, words, and actions. Without self-discipline, success is impossible, period. Discipline is doing what needs to get done even when you do not feel like it. When you are undisciplined, you become a slave to your moods, appetites, and selfish ways. Disciplining the flesh is one of the hardest things you will ever do. Train your mind not to indulge. We repeat what we will not repair. We all can get upset. Our goal is to remain self-controlled. This is a fruit of the Holy Spirit. You have a responsibility to God and yourself to operate from the Holy Spirit. Or just stay stuck. Self-discipline is preparation for growth. I believe self-discipline is the true definition of loving God and yourself. Even physical fitness is a spiritual discipline. Good health honors God. Discipline is freedom. It all starts with self-love. You can control your flesh, or it will control you. But afterwards, there will be a peaceful harvest of right living for those who are trained in this way. Discipline is wisdom. I know people who endure difficult situations for a long period of time, and they have the most disciplined, beautiful attitudes. This is a wonderful example to us all.

I declare: "I operate in self-control. Self-control and discipline add protection to my life."

JUNE 26

Do not get fooled by the energy around you. You have the power of the Holy Spirit to influence the energy. When you know you are loved completely by God, not one person can make you feel worthless. Do not stoop down to fit in places you have outgrown. Learn to avoid three shapes: vicious circles, love triangles, and squared minds. Do not chase attention. Biblical love is not emotions or feelings. It is an attitude to seek the best interest of the other person regardless of how you feel towards them. You can eat all the kale, purchase anything you want, and take the most amazing trips, but if you do not rest your soul in Jesus and become like Him, you will never find purpose or peace. Be good to others for just no reason. Grow from the dirt that is thrown at you. Know the power of God. Know your worth. Never believe you are above or below. Stay humble. Listen to no man who does not listen to God. We talk about things we think of the most. Declare: It is my season. God will make it happen. Do something that will lead you closer to God! No assignment is more important than another; we are all needed to accomplish God's perfect will. Do what you are called to do.

I declare: "It is my season; God will make it happen!"

J U N E   2 7

A grateful heart protects you from negative thinking. You can control the quality of your life. My favorite age is *now*. You cannot control how others see you or think about you. Guess what? You need to get comfortable with that. Growing up is optional. Growing old is a choice. Age is unstoppable. Think about how many seasons you have seen change. How many hearts have you loved? How many concerts have you been to? How many trips have you taken? How many holidays have you celebrated? That is your age! As you grow older, it is all about the person you have become! Your real beauty has no expiration date. I am a born survivor. I am extremely grateful for the years that have passed by. Live your life and forget that age. We grow old by our thoughts. Today is the oldest you have ever been and the youngest you will ever be again. God is saying to you today you have not seen your best days yet. God specializes in the impossible. Beautiful older people are works of art. Put God *first*, and just watch your life change. God selected you. Love yourself! Age, distance, height, and weight are just numbers. Change will not happen overnight; invest in yourself.

I declare: "By Your favor, Lord, You have established me as a strong mountain."

JUNE 28

You will not be able to control what is happening; the way you respond will make it work out. It is time to be happy. Other emotions, such as anger, sadness, being overwhelmed, or over-thinking, are seriously just not worth it. *Overthinking* kills your positive mindset. Today declare: I refuse to stress myself out about all the things that I cannot control. Calmness is from the hand of the Master. Do not allow others to control the direction of your life because the Bible says your footsteps are ordered from the Lord. We fall, we break, and we fail. But God lifts us up and heals us. We are overcomers. You will have good days, bad days, overwhelming days, and amazing days. But the best day, no matter what, is the day you woke up. Your family is priceless. Your time is gold. And your health is your true wealth. Health shows you how rich you really are. Get so full of the Holy Spirit that even if they take and take and take, you will still be overflowing in the anointing. Welcome back. No one is you, and that is your power. Today, I will not stress over things I cannot control. If someone makes you happy, make them happier.

I declare: "I refuse to stress myself out about all the things that I cannot control."

JUNE 29

It is very important to just let go and let meekness, humbleness, and loveliness separate you from that stubborn flesh. This will free you from the power of the devil. The Word of God is so powerful, sharper than a two-edged sword. It will pierce your heart; it will help discipline your thoughts and the intents of your heart (Hebrews 4:12). God cannot use you if you do not nail that flesh to the cross. Let it all go: God will take care of you. The plan over your life is to serve others, not self-serve yourself. The way of the world now, everywhere you go, is self-service. Selfies, selfishness, self, all about you is a trick from the enemy. Be careful. The Word of God is powerful and the same, whether you believe it or not. You will pick what you plant; stay humble. Unselfishly seek the best for one another, just as Christ has loved you. No greater love than to lay down your own life for your friends and family.

I declare: "I am not selfish and self-centered; I deny myself; I take up my cross and follow Jesus. I forget myself, lose sight of myself and all my own interests (Matthew 16:24)."

JUNE 30

Faith is the down payment for your future. Start thinking you are blessed. Talk like you are blessed. Act like you are blessed. This is how you activate your faith. It is easy to spot a yellow car when you are always thinking of a yellow car. You become what you constantly think about. Work on your habits, mindset, and healing your past. Sometimes, you must change your environment to grow. Detox your phone, your page, your home, your counters, your closet, your car, and your mind. You know what your business is? It is how you speak to yourself. Sometimes, the best therapy is a drive with praise music. During hard times do not pull away. There is something very calming to look up and see a billion stars at night and realize they are held together by God, who knows exactly what He is doing. God is arranging things for you even when you do not see a way.

I declare: "My faith does not rest in the wisdom of men [human philosophy] but in the power of God" (1 Corinthians 2:5, NKJV; paraphrased).

July

What goes into someone's mouth does not defile them, but what comes out of their mouth, that is what defiles them.

Matthew 15:11 (NIV)

Your words are powerful. Be careful what you speak.

JULY 1

Just think, the King of this universe calls you His prized possession! For God has not given you the spirit of fear. He has given you power and love and a peaceful mind (2 Timothy 1:7). "Holy Spirit, move in my life. Take over my heart. Be over my family. Launch my dreams. Bless me with whatever You have for me." It is so nice to wake up in the morning knowing that God has blessed you with another day. I believe in God. Not because my parents told me but because I have experienced struggle and saw how amazing He truly is. I can rest in the fact that God is in control. The enemy will always try to limit you in praying. Why? Because that devil knows your praying will limit him. Get praying. Prayer will always be your most important conversation of the day. Take it to God first. The devil does not care if you read your Bible or not. He just does not want you to apply the blood of Christ and the powerful Word over your life. Speak it out loud now over yourself, the Word! Your purpose is to please God, not others. Keep the enemy out.

I declare: "I submit myself to God, I resist the devil, and He must flee."

JULY 2

God has another win in store for you. You must not let evil conquer you but conquer evil by always doing good. A more than a conqueror attitude is when you have a lot to say, but you choose to remain silent in front of naysayers. Do not be overcome by evil but overcome evil with your goodness. Behind every strong person lies a broken person who had to learn how to get up and totally depend on God. Find someone who loves you unconditionally, respects you, cares for you, and does not want to lose you. There is healing in praise music, sitting at the ocean, and staring at the stars. God is involved in them all. You get what you work for. You are important, and you exist for a God-given purpose. Be that person you want to have in your life. Until you spread your wings, you will have no idea how far you can really fly.

I declare: "It is my winning season."

JULY 3

I could send you a million motivational quotes. I also could show you testimonials of "before and afters" from reading your Bible. I can show you beautiful meals of just good ole health. The truth is you are the one that needs to want the change. Do you have time to worry, doubt, fear, and rehearse the curse, murmur, and complain? Well, then you have time to set new goals, pray, prioritize sleep, work out, read faith-filled books, and listen to faith-filled sermons for you to grow. You always have been beautiful and handsome. But now you are deciding to be spiritually mature and fit, healthier, stronger, kinder, and living a victorious life that you choose. The life God gave us is amazing. By taking care of our temples, we will feel fantastic. Be stronger than all your excuses. I am happier when I feel healthier: mind, body, and soul. It is a lifestyle.

I declare: "I set my mind and keep it set on what is above (the higher things), not on the things that are on the earth (Colossians 3:2)."

JULY 4

Becoming strong does not start in the gym; it starts in your mind. Put this right in your mind; you must be filled with the Holy Spirit to keep the mind strong and be safeguarded by the Word of God. You will not have to be an extreme person to change your life. Just consistent. Be willing to start over every morning. "Seek ye first the kingdom of God..." (Matthew 6:33a, KJV) Purpose will be your alarm clock. It is your will, not your skills. Just look in the mirror and see your competition. Every failure has a blessing attached to it. Do not get discouraged if you are not where you thought you would be! Consistency does not mean perfect. Life is a one-time offer; use it well. Pray. He listens. I asked God to help me grow. And it started to rain. It is about what you learn during the pain. I have God-confidence. When prayer is your habit, you can expect miracles. Reach a place, and do not let anyone or anything interfere with the plan of God. Stand on the Word.

I declare: "The Lord makes me have a surplus of prosperity through the fruit of my body. He blesses me in the land that He gives me."

JULY 5

Aging is just another word for living. The secret to aging beautifully is to enjoy every second of it. Your heart will never have wrinkles. Mindfulness, positivity, and positive affirmations reveal your inner beauty that has no age. Love is timeless, ageless, and endless. A loyal heart is precious. It is a lack of friendship that starts the problem. A joyful spirit will always stay youthful. Real God's love does not meet you at your best. It always meets you in your mess. The older I get, I cannot care what others think of me; therefore, I certainly enjoy myself. For the Word says, "[...] I am fearfully and wonderfully made" (Psalm 139:14a, NKJV). And so are you. Remember, handwritten love letters will never go out of style. Timeless love is never old. Neither are old-school picnics, real phone calls, flowers, date nights, and late-night drives. And I believe, most importantly, that you cannot break a person who gets their strength for seeking God first thing. Age well and live your purpose of life.

I declare: "I will hear and receive Your sayings, and the years of my life will be many."

JULY 6

Just remember that one time you prayed, dreamed, and planned of being where you are right now! Be a helper, a hugger, and a friendly face, and you can make the world a better place. Keep life simple. Enjoy those little things. Life only gets better when you do. You seriously do not have to be perfect. Sometimes, it is the simple little conversations that mean more. The happiest people do not have the best of everything; they have learned to make the best out of every situation. It is a true blessing to live like that. You are the one that creates beautiful opportunities. Stay aware. A strong person can wake up and start smiling because they are going to pray their way through the day. God will put you right back together in front of the people that broke you. All things work together for the good for those who keep their trust in God!

I declare: "I give thanks to the Lord for His unfailing love and His wonderful deeds for me, for He satisfies the thirsty and fills the hungry with good things (Psalm 107:8)."

JULY 7

One of the best gifts is permission to feel beautiful in one's own skin. To feel loved. To feel valuable. To feel like we are more than enough. You do not just wake up and become a butterfly. Growth is a process. Ask yourself every morning, "What am I going to pay attention to today? Am I going to focus on the positive to move my life forward in what God has planned for me?" You must teach your mindset to grow in a positive direction. Find your "who"; nothing will work unless you do. Find your strengths. You are already good enough. Everything is going to be okay. God says it is time to receive something you have been asking for by faith. Most of the stuff you worry about will not happen anyway. Mindset is everything. Gratefulness turns what we have into more than enough. Do not let weekends be your "weak ends." Stay strong. Trust God. Believe always that something good is about to happen. Celebrate every single day. You can. Spend time with people you love. Daily reminder: You are more than enough. If God is for you, who can be against you? Stay close to God for your job, the person you marry, where you live, and what you do. It will work out perfectly even if it does not appear so now.

I declare: "The Lord loves those who love Him, and those who seek Him early and diligently shall find Him (Proverbs 8:17)."

JULY 8

Problems will always shout for your attention! This is for you! "Stop monitoring things you left in My hands! Trust Me and rest!" The Holy Spirit has been showing me to stop worrying, to stop overthinking, to stop the fear of what others think; stop thinking He will not answer your prayers. He is saying, today, to put your trust in only Him. Help others who the Lord puts on your heart! Stay thankful and grateful and worship Him during the storm. And in due season, you will reap your answers. He has the plan and holds the key to your future. I am waiting for Him to show me the way! Until then, I am going to keep on praising Him. You can do it! A healthy person understands that the negative actions of others have nothing to do with him. Each day, you get to decide which person you will be. The choice is yours. I thank God for life and all the lessons. I am not perfect at all, but I am happy.

I declare: "I am not afraid of receiving bad news; my faith is strong, and I trust in the Lord. I am not worried or afraid (Psalm 112:7)."

JULY 9

We need practice and experience with our faith. So, if you are in a tough season, resist the temptation to give up. If we hang in there and refuse to give up on our faith in God, we will be more than the devil can handle. After I had gone through a series of failures, shame, divorce, insecurity, and guilt, I did not know how my future would turn out. I knew I needed to break free from some negative habits, negative cycles, and negative people. When I got desperate enough and sought the Lord earnestly and daily, "ah," my life started to change. God restored my life. I encourage you today to break free from the cycle of poor, negative choices. Now. Stop murmuring, complaining, and rehearsing your past. That will keep you down and make you feel more like a failure. The victim mentality must stop. You are a victorious person. With the help of the Holy Spirit, you can make your dreams real. People are amazed when I share my messed-up testimony and show them how God has changed me from the inside out. Daily reading of faith-filled books, listening to faith-filled messages, praying, asking, and believing God for the outcome have changed me. God is a respecter of no person, and if He changed me, He could change you. I am encouraging you. You are not alone.

I declare: "I have victory everywhere I go."

JULY 10

Switch on the positive mindset. It is all up to you. The *one* you feed wins! There are two spirits inside of you, the flesh and the Holy Spirit. They will always be fighting; one is darkness, despair, hate, anger, and jealousy. The other is light, hope, love, joy, peace, and truth of God's Word. This battle rages daily within you. I thought to myself for a moment, Which spirit will "win"? The Holy Spirit showed me the spirit that wins daily is the one you feed daily. Stop trying to figure out what others think. You are not a crystal ball. Stop trying to control the outcome of circumstances. God is in control. And mind your business and work on being a better you. God wants us to be *salt* and *light*, no matter what. You have got to find people who love like you do. You cannot change those around you at all. Do not be a fault finder. Never treat others badly. Treat them like you expect to be treated. Do not see a mask; look for the soul. Your job is to be a soul seeker to build God's Kingdom. I will not give anyone a reason to hate me. Happy life: destroy negative limiting beliefs. Trust God and do good always. That is the Word!

I declare:

As a disciple of Christ, I have the keys of the kingdom of heaven; and whatever I bind on earth is bound and whatever I loose is loosed in heaven.

Matthew 16:19 (NKJV; paraphrased)

JULY 11

This is your timeline; you are not off schedule. Check your-self. Do better, be better. Take a deep breath. Pause whenever you are about to act hardcore of things you may regret. Know your own value. Show kindness to unkind people. Forgive others who may have hurt you. Do not be with people who criticize you. The day I changed was the day I quit trying to fit into a worldview that did not fit me. Do not let evil conquer you; conquer evil by doing good. Joyfulness is your key. Your entire house is about to get blessed. God says to trust Him and be a good doer of the Word. Be good to others for no reason. When God steps in, miracles happen. I am the kind of queen that knows my crown is not on my head but in my soul. I am a soul seeker and a Kingdom builder. This is an awesome privilege. My future is in the hands of God!

I declare: "I am rooted, established, strong, immovable, and determined."

JULY 12

We all can get stuck in negative self-talk. Challenge yourself. Accept and love the things that may give you doubt. You cannot tell others how to feel unless you are them. God will always cause you to triumph. Cleanse yourself of all feelings of selfishness, self-condemnation, and misinterpretation of your experiences. Declare: I am fearfully and wonderfully made, I am blessed, I am valuable, I am directed by the Holy Spirit. I am joyful; I am loved; I am happy; I am confident; I am me. God made me who I am. I am a beautiful believer.

I am unique. I am gifted. "Lord, as I begin my day, I pray that You would fill me with Your Holy Spirit. Cover me with Your protection from spiritual attacks. Help me to speak only the words You would have me speak. In Jesus' name, I ask."

I declare: "I am fearfully and wonderfully made; I am blessed; I am valuable; I am directed by the Holy Spirit."

JULY 13

My family is not perfect, but they are perfect for me. There is no place like where you are at right now. Grateful and thankful. What do you think is stopping you from living your best life? The best things in life are free. Start today, staying thankful for each family member. We all have differences; celebrate them. Each person brings something unique and beautiful to the table. Switch on your positive mindset. Anyone can think negatively or speak negative news. Be the difference for the good. We all have twenty-four hours in a day, but it is your choice what you do with them. Kick it up a notch. Do something that your future self will thank you for. Or ten years from now, you will be in the same place. It all starts with a decision. Life waits for no one. You only have the present, which is the most beautiful gift. "Lord, I declare that You will put on my heart and show me what I need to eliminate from my life that holds me back to be all I can be. Show me Your plan over my life, my future, and for my family." Family is the greatest gift! Inspire all our differences to make a beautiful life to share together.

I declare: "I leave my troubles with the Lord, and He will defend me; He never lets honest people be defeated."

JULY 14

There is always something to be thankful for. Start the habit of asking yourself, "Does what I am thinking and speaking support the life I am praying and believing for?" God is getting ready to unleash a double portion of blessings of favor over your life: over all the trials, setbacks, headaches, and tests that you have endured. God has a major life-changing blessing just for you. Do not give up. Walk in love. Walk by faith. Stay in forgiveness and joyfulness. Do not squeeze out the Holy Spirit's power by your thinking or behavior. The Lord looks at the heart. He has made everything beautiful in its time. There is a time for every season. For God has not given us the spirit of fear, but of power and of love and a sound mind (2 Timothy 1:7). Therefore, do not worry about tomorrow.

I declare: "God has given me one new commandment that I should love others just as He has loved me."

JULY 15

It always happens when you feel hopeless and discouraged; the enemy will whisper, "You might as well give up; things will never change." If you believe this huge lie, you will not believe God's promises, and you may stop praying. You can be revived! Obedience is the key; do not be fooled. Keeping your mouth filled with *life-giving* words from God's Word is so vital to your breakthrough. Zipper up! I declare that all things work together for those who put their trust in God. No weapon formed against me shall prosper in Jesus' name. Negative energy cannot stay. I release it and send it away in Jesus' name. I am choosing now to release myself from thoughts that do not bless me or others. I declare I am filled with Holy Spirit growth, positive change, healing, and agape love, with supernatural breakthroughs. This is the day the Lord has made—I am rejoicing and will stay glad (Psalm 118:24)! I am just a vessel for God! God is on your side. God is in control, and His ways and timing are perfect. He is the Lord of *life*.

I declare: "I am filled with Holy Spirit growth, positive change, healing, and agape love with supernatural breakthroughs."

JULY 16

Texting while driving is the hot topic these days! But ask yourself this. The Bible says, "Serve the Lord without distraction" (1 Corinthians 7:35b, NKJV). In other words, keep your eyes on Him and not on others. This is called staying on the highway of holiness. It is no different when you get behind the wheel of a car. Many of our distractions in life are caused by our selfish fleshly desires gathered by our enemy, the devil. So, if you are distracted in life or when driving, be aware of the importance to keeping your eyes on the road and your hands on the wheel for the safety of all of us. No different than keeping your eyes on the Word and being a hearer and a doer of the Word for the safety of all of us in this life. Living *life* to the fullest. No distractions. Look away from all that tries to distract you from living your best life. Do not get bewitched; the enemy is out there prowling around to see who he can fool. Do not let anybody steal your crown. You are a child of the King of kings.

I declare: "I am very, very careful never to compromise with the people around me, and I do not follow their evil ways."

JULY 17

How are you using your mouth? The Lord wants us to use it to speak with love, show joy, help the weak, and strengthen them with words of encouragement. It is not right, nor is it acceptable to the Lord, to use our mouth to bring hatred, to say hurtful things, or to show destruction. The Bible instructs us not to go against the Holy Spirit. Do not let any unwholesome, profane, worthless words ever come out of your mouth. Only use words for building up others, not bullying. We are to use our words for blessing up others. What are you saying? Are you building up or tearing down? Choose your words wisely and speak with agreement out of the Word of God. Jesus gives us inspiration and instruction on how to handle our mouths. Hearing the Word is great, but we need to be doers of His Word daily. You cannot control others. So, let them have their opinions. *Focus* on doing God's will. A time to keep quiet? When you are under emotional emergency, sometimes, the best thing to do is to keep quiet. Do not let the enemy work through you and make that bad situation worse. Words are extremely powerful. Choose yours wisely. Be a hope dealer.

I declare: "When I walk in love, God is present."

JULY 18

It does not matter if the glass is half empty or half full, be grateful you have a glass and there is something in it. Life is not perfect. Stay grateful for everything you do have. You were born to be real, not perfect. Imperfections are beautiful. A beautiful thing is never perfect. Do not get fooled by what you think you see. It takes a huge amount of hard work to make life beautiful in all areas. I get it; as I live longer, my imperfections are everything. Plus, imperfections make things much more interesting. No beauty shines brighter than that of a good heart. Spiritual maturity goes right along with healthy communication. Your mind and your words are a garden. You choose what kind of seeds to plant in them. You can spend time taking care of others' gardens. Or you can work on making your garden awesome and attract other awesome people to your garden. Do not keep habits that are draining: taking things personally, past failures, poor diet, complaining, overthinking, or people-pleasing. Face it until you make it all great. Be so by building a beautiful thinking life so you have no time to doubt, worry, fear, or hate. God came to show us the abundant life by walking in love.

I declare:

I am like a tree firmly planted by the streams of water, ready to bring forth its fruit in its season; its leaf also shall not fade or wither; and everything I do shall prosper [and come to maturity].

Psalm 1:3 (NIV; paraphrased)

JULY 19

As you begin this day, start right away saying beautiful things, and you will see your whole day change for the better. Stay away from toxic words; they damage your brain. Using words to tear apart others is not from God. You can change the direction of your day by what *you say*. Today, I want to encourage you to seek forgiveness, to use right words, and to be very careful what you speak. Out of the same mouth can come both blessings and cursing. We have a responsibility to our souls to choose blessings. You can help or harm. You will not be able to tame your tongue without the help of God. Pray and ask the Lord to help you to use the words of your mouth to speak encouragement and blessings to yourself and others. Submit to the authority of God and resist the devil. Stand firm against him, and he will flee. Your mouth is a key that can unlock and unleash blessings or cursing. Humble yourself; do not slander or judge. There is only one Judge, and that is God. We are to be salt and light. Anytime the enemy attacks your mind, just remember the battle belongs to the Lord.

I declare:

If you [I] forgive men their trespasses [their reckless and willful sins, leaving them, letting them go, and giving up resentment], your [my] heavenly Father will also forgive you [me].

Matthew 6:14 (NKJV)

JULY 20

I love this: The devil saw me with my head down and thought he had won. Until I said, *"Amen!"* Hallelujah. Stay strong, have faith, and trust God. You are going to make it. Others do not realize the strength it takes to pull your own self by praying out of a dark place mentally. If you did that today or any other day, I give God the glory for you. Breathe; you are going to be okay. Some days, it takes a lot of work just to be okay. I get it. You are still strong. Do not stop. You must keep on going. God is not asking you to figure it out or fix it. God is asking you to trust Him for what He has for you. Your wound is probably not your fault, but praying and declaring His Word for your healing is your responsibility. Declare: "Holy Spirit, energize me for Your work. My body is Yours. My mind is Yours. I know You will be faithful to complete the good work You have started in me. Great is Your faithfulness over my failures. My future is in Your hands. I trust You fully. In Jesus' name."

I declare: "Holy Spirit, energize me for Your work. My body and mind are Yours. I know You will be faithful to complete the good work You began."

JULY 21

The devil seeks to defeat you daily by making you trust your own wisdom. Trust God. The Holy Spirit will guide you into truth. Every single great moment and movement of God can be traced back to a kneeling person. The Bible? It is not just a book on how to walk in love and be a nice forgiving person. It is your *greatest weapon* of warfare, offensive weapon against the devil in your spiritual war. Read Ephesians 6:10–20 out loud. Discipline is doing what needs to be done, even if you do not want to do it. The devil will try to destroy your mind. *But God* is about to give you a mind-blowing breakthrough. Before you open yourself to someone, ask God to reveal their true character. God will do it, and when He does, stop making excuses.

I declare: "I set my mind and keep it set on what is above (the higher things), not on the things that are on earth."

JULY 22

Make that decision to get back up, and do not get discouraged. Ask yourself, "Am I going to start again or give up?" No one is perfect! Perfect love casts out fear. Whatever you have written down for your goals, I declare, and in agreement, success is yours in Jesus' name. Whatever situations you are dealing with, I declare you will overcome them. Declare: I am blessed, balanced, and peaceful in every way today. In Jesus' name. All those things you are overthinking, God is already working on them. Stay in <u>praise</u>. The key is to keep on doing the right thing. Do not take things in your own hands. What is meant for your harm will be turned around for your advantage. It is in God's Word. When you have a goal, you have work to do. No excuses.

I declare: "I am blessed, balanced, and peaceful in every way 'today.'"

JULY 23

The day will come when every person stands before God and give an account of his or her life. This is one truth none will be able to avoid. It is time to give others and us a break. Why do we get so frustrated when others say things about us, when we say things about others? It is just time to take a step back and give others the break we so gracefully give ourselves. This is called spiritual maturity. God's way is right. He tells us to forgive others, turn the other cheek, and pray for those who despitefully use us. We need to give others the same mercy as we give ourselves and the ones dear to us. His Kingdom is unshakable. His love is undeniable. What are we doing with our example to others? Be the person you want to meet. Be the person you want to live with. Be the person you want to work with. Be the person you want as a friend. Declare: I want to be that person who forgives quickly, who shows patience, loves, and who is there for others. I know it can be exhausting being positive. But I want to encourage you; it is so worth it! On that special day, there will be no excuses. The time is now to be all God created you to be.

I declare: "God disciplines me for my certain good that I might become a partaker of His holiness."

JULY 24

You are unique, and so am I. That is what makes us better and stronger together. No toxic thinking; it damages your brain. Do not let the silly little things steal your happiness. Be very careful what you think about. Your thoughts run your life. So that means they can ruin your life too. Do not say things that are not true. Keep your eyes focused on what is right. It is okay to vent, just do not vent the same thing over and over to everyone you meet. Be honest with yourself. If you know you need to do better, then do better. Stop blaming circumstances. It is your job to adapt. Rebuild yourself in private. Do not feel guilty if you are not doing your best today. Be strong in the moments you are feeling weak. Be a student of life, always learning. Every experience is from God. This is preparation for our future that only He can see. Walking by faith. Be a warrior, not a worrier. Be that reason someone believes in the goodness of God. Do not ignore your own potential. It is a gift from God. God is in control, and He knows what He is doing.

I declare: "As I think in my heart, so am I."

JULY 25

When you think you have used all possibilities up, remember that you have not. Stop stressing. If God wants someone in your life, He will pave the way. You will not have to make it happen yourself. Stop negative thinking. And you cannot do this while having mental chatter. Humble is your new word. You owe it to yourself to become everything you are dreaming of. Train your mind to see God in all you do. Start counting your blessings. Declare: I am fearless. In the middle of an ordinary day, something you prayed for will show up. The Lord has you on His mind. Keep the shield of faith. Healing comes from the things you do not negatively speak about. I love positive people. I am an imperfect person loved by a perfect God, and so are you. The toughest opponent of all is the one inside your head. God knew you before He formed you and put you in your mother's womb (Jeremiah 1:5). He set you apart.

I declare: "I am fearless!"

JULY 26

Feel the feeling but do not become the emotion. Release it.

Your greatest mistake? Living in fear that you will make one. Sometimes, if others cannot find anything wrong with you, they may create something! You were born to make mistakes, not to fake it. Persist until you succeed. Pray like Nehemiah. Serve like Martha. Believe like Mary. Build like Noah. And we do know that in all things, God works for the good of those who love Him (Romans 8:28). Love like Jesus. Clothe yourself with a gentle and quiet spirit, which is so precious to God. We all have days where we feel like we cannot make it. Dreams are shattered. Friends leave. Family hurt us. Sickness fears us. But God will always guide us and see us through. Today is not the day to lose hope. Have faith to hold on to hope. Trust in God always. Feeling stuck? Your limitations of faith may be holding you back. Sometimes, we need to thank God for what has not happened.

I declare: "I live before God, doing my duty with a perfectly good conscience."

JULY 27

Some days, you just have to dance and shake off fear and disappointment when life around you seems to be out of control. Your disappointments do not dictate God's unconditional love. You can tell a lot about a person by what they choose to see in you. If others talk about you, it is because if they talked about themselves, no one would listen. Become that friend you pray for. You will attract what you are! Being beautiful is when you have a lot to say, but you choose to remain silent. Invest in yourself because you are so worth it. Negativity is sneaky. I can multitask, listen, be silent, and *forget* all at the same time. It is a gift from God. The Lord sees your heart. Anyone that kneels before God can stand before anyone. The best way to keep the enemy out is to keep Christ in. God allows difficulties to help us grow. I am growing.

I declare: "I am determined and confident! I am not afraid or discouraged, for the Lord my God is with me wherever I go (Joshua 1:9)."

JULY 28

You will make it, and this will make you stronger. You cannot understand a pain you have not endured. Focus on growth: your heart, your soul, and your mind. God's got the rest. Pray because when we pray for each other, something *supernatural* takes place. Take a moment and pray for the person on your heart. Prayer time has no expiration date. Note to self: I will pray for those who have hurt me. Pray continually. Today, think about all that you are instead of all that you are not. Celebrate success of who you are. And give others permission to go for their dreams. Let others be inspired by how you deal with your imperfections. What do you need to start doing today to end this year successfully?

I declare: "Fear has no grip on me."

JULY 29

Look at the bigger picture. Breathe! Feeling distracted and overwhelmed? Ask God to help you learn lessons from the circumstances which you feel overwhelmed in. You know God is drawing us closer to Him through all of this. You also are experiencing sustaining power from God. Learn everything you can. This will not last. Remember all the beautiful things God has taught you through some other painful experiences you thought you would never survive. You were born to be an overcomer. Endings are always new beginnings to God! Trust the process. Delight yourself in the Lord, and He will give you the desires of your heart. If God is for you, then who can be against you? No one can stop the plan that God has for you. God can change your status. God can give you that job. God can make a way out of no way. God can put a light on top of a mountain. God could put a stream in a desert. Only God. I am asking You today, Lord, to teach my heart what breaks Your heart. I desire to be like You! God holds the keys to life and death. Look at the bigger picture.

I declare: "This is my comfort and consolation in my affliction: Your word has revived me and given me life."

JULY 30

Access opened to the enemy by judging and criticizing others. Anyplace that you do not have a responsibility in, be alert and smart not to offer your opinion. We need to practice not judging or criticizing others. Focus less on what we think our opinion is of others' shortcomings. When you judge, you open the door for an attack from the enemy. We need to examine what is wrong with us. Deny the information and influence from the enemy, and do not give him an opportunity to squeeze in your mind and confuse it. He is the father of all lies, confusion, anger, resentment, judgmental spirit, and strong condemnation.

I declare: "I will seek 'first' God's Kingdom and His righteousness. Then everything else I need to handle others will be given to me also."

JULY 31

Sometimes, the littlest things take up the most room in your heart. Everything will shift when you replace the words, "Why is this happening to me?" with, "What beautiful thing am I learning from this?" Everything will shift. Stay real. Just master this day. Pray for grace. Not fitting in can be one of your best qualities. A healed person understands. An unhealed person can find offense with pretty much anything someone does. Your compassion for others reflects how powerful your agape love is from the Holy Spirit. Privacy is power. Notice everything but keep your mouth shut. Silence cannot be misquoted. God has the perfect plan. Worry increases pressure, but prayer releases peace. Never stop praying. God is the best listener. God works in His timing. If you need someone just to listen, then just pray. Overwhelmed, overthinking? Pray.

I declare: "I am growing and becoming strong in spirit, filled with wisdom, and the grace (favor and spiritual blessing) of God is upon me."

August

*From the fruit of their mouth a person's stomach is filled;
with the harvest of their lips they are satisfied. The tongue
has the power of life and death, and those who love it will eat
its fruit.*

Proverbs 18:20–21 (NIV)

Your words are powerful. Be careful what you speak.

AUGUST 1

You are not too broken for the grace of Jesus. Because God is your strength (Habakkuk 3:17). Science says that you need four basic elements to survive: water, air, food, and light. Look what the Bible says about Jesus: He is the Living Water. He is the Breath of Life. He is the Bread of Life. He is the Light of the World. Science is right; we need Jesus to survive. "I knew you before I formed you in your mother's womb. Before you were born, I set you apart..." (Jeremiah 1:5a, NIV; paraphrased) Pray continually. The Holy Spirit will help you pray (Romans 8:26–27). Stay calm, comfortable, be encouraging, enlightening, lead others, and reassure them that God loves them. Do not worry, obsess, condemn, discourage, confuse, push, or live in fear, and do not rush; this is not the voice of God. He knows the plans for you (Jeremiah 29:11). Keep reminding yourself that changes take time; each day you work on yourself, the structure of your brain will be transformed for the better. But it will take time. Be patient with yourself. With the help and guidance of the Holy Spirit, we can change the structure of our brains.

I declare: "God is my strength, my rock, and my salvation. God is the source of all life."

AUGUST 2

No matter what today you are facing, the Lord *can* handle it. Going to the Word of God for His wisdom is a wise choice. Or you can stay stuck in your overthinking and overwhelming problems. Be careful who you allow to explain what you are going through. Your only choice may be that you decide to do things in your own abilities! The Lord will use the adversity, but only to make you look to the Father and His Word for the true answers. "Oh, that My people would listen to Me, [...] with honey from the rock I would have satisfied you" (Psalm 81:13a, 16b, NKJV). Who are you listening to? Your choice. This can build you up or tear you down. You have a choice in the matter. Scripture is clear; if you ask, you will receive (Matthew 7:7). God has a plan; it is all about pushing you to get out of the old way of thinking and not to stay stuck. He is about being intentional for the new decade. *Push* right now and birth that dream. May I ask why you are waiting? The life clock is ticking away. You have so much to do for Him. Live like people so inspired.

I declare: "I will seek the Lord for answers and wait for His reply."

AUGUST 3

Declare: I am walking in victory. I have got my joy back.

Lord led me because I cannot do this life alone. Tears are prayers that travel to God when we can't speak. Write out Psalm 118:29. Pray to forgive when you cannot forget. Do not panic. Each day has a purpose. God created you with a longing in your heart that only He can fill. Nothing that is happening is a surprise to God. He knows all about it. Satan's target is your mind, and his weapons are lies. Fill your mind with God's Word. Those that sow in tears shall reap with joy. See life as possibilities, not problems. No risk; no testimony.

Positivity is a superpower. *Praying* is supernatural. Kindness is a *power*. Just work super hard. Make an impact in your circle. Be you; an original is worth more than a copy. Say prayers, set goals, and work hard. Think of the countless blessings God gave you without asking! When you feel poisoned by pain, fear, stress, pressure, or people-pleasing, the best antidote is to *pray*. Nothing more, nothing less. It is supernatural.

I declare: "I am walking in victory. I have got my joy back. God is doing great work in me. Kingdom 'thinker'!"

AUGUST 4

Fear is a liar! Your greatest test this year will be how you handle people who have mishandled you. My response to every situation is, "It is all good," because even if it isn't, I am making sure it will be. Who is with me on this? It is your story. Feel free to hit them up with a plot twist. Do not claim you are praying to grow and then run away the minute you feel the growing pains. One more thought, stop expecting people who see you as a threat to give you support. Beautiful is the man who does not ignore the woman he cares about. An unhealed person can find offense in pretty much anything someone does. A healed person understands the actions of others have nothing to do with them. Be concerned about what is inside of a person, not their model looks. No matter how tough everything becomes, you must never run out of sweetness. A beautiful goal is to make people feel good about themselves. Your beauty should not come from outward adornment. Rather, it should be that of your inner self, the unfading beauty of a gentle and quiet spirit, which is of great worth in God's sight (1 Peter 3:3–4). Never get disappointed.

I declare: "I will love others as God loves me, regardless of how I am treated."

AUGUST 5

When I stopped venting and started praying, my life changed. I found out you do not need sympathy; you need strength. Bruised, not broken. Reminding myself daily that everything is not perfect; just look for authenticity and sincerity. Speak to others as if they were the wisest, most beautiful, most important, lovely human beings on Earth. For what they hear, they will believe, and they will become. Start with yourself, your mate, and your children. It would be nice if everyone you worked with spoke this way. You be the trendsetter. Declare: I am spiritually, emotionally, and physically ready to enter this new phase in my life. I am ready to grow. I am ready to get better. The negativity of others or of this world cannot pull me down unless I allow it to poison my mind. Let that sink in. Do not forget to pray when things are going well too. The God who created the most magnificent sights on Earth also created me. I. Love. This.

I declare: "I am spiritually, emotionally, and physically ready to enter this new phase in my life. I am ready to grow. I am ready to get better."

AUGUST 6

Softness is a great strength. It is the lack of communication that ruins things. Kindness is free. Sprinkle that stuff everywhere you go today. A true mark of maturity is when someone hurts you, and you try to understand their circumstances rather than hurt them back. That is emotional maturity. Everyone is growing old, but not everyone is growing up. The way you communicate, the way you consider others, the way you understand others, the way you see things, the way you react, and value things represents yourself as a mature adult. Or not. Maturity does not always come with age. Keep moving forward. Know your worth. Just because you are offended does not mean you are right. Maturity is when you have power to destroy someone who wronged you, but you breathe instead and walk away, staying joyful. You know God's got it. Trust in God always. Let Him deal with them. Read Galatians 6:1–10, and sow good seeds.

I declare: "Do not be deceived: God cannot be mocked. A man reaps what he sows" (Galatians 6:7, NIV).

AUGUST 7

Your power is the *key* to spiritual healing and maturity.

Praise is a weapon. Worship is a weapon. Prayer is a weapon. The devil hates them all. He wants us to murmur and complain like spoiled children that must get their way. This is exactly what keeps us stuck in the pointless poison in our minds. It is powerless, and the enemy loves it. It is a tool he uses for defeat to destroy our mind, body, and soul. That is why the Bible refers to the enemy as the father of all lies. We become a puppet for the enemy against our own souls. Be aware the enemy walks around like a roaring lion to seek whom he can devour (1 Peter 5:8). Protect your mind with the Word. Speak from the Word. Declare your affirmations from the Word. If God is for me, who can be against me? Before you were ever born, God had a purpose for you. Whine or shine; the choice is yours. This can be used for your spiritual growth chart.

I declare: "Do not be anxious about anything, [...] by prayer and petition, with thanksgiving, present your requests to God" (Philippians 4:6, NIV).

AUGUST 8

Do you notice that you glow differently when you are happy? Train yourself to cultivate a thankful mindset! You do not need social approval to be happy. I found someone I never want to lose again, and that is me. Do not lose yourself trying to keep everyone else happy. Challenge yourself to love the things that give you doubt. This current situation is giving you a golden opportunity to re-evaluate what you need. Three months from now, you will thank yourself. You owe yourself the love you freely give to others. Give yourself the pep talk. Keep taking time for yourself until you are you again. The reason why you are tired is you allow storms to disrupt you. When really, they have come to clear your path to your destiny. Are you ready for that new chapter? What God has for you is for you. Timing is everything. Trust His plan. His plan is greater than our plan every time. Stop comparing. Faith in God includes faith in His timing. If it does not open, it is not your door. Happiness is a key to gratitude, and the Holy Spirit resonates when you remain joyful. God will open up the way before you, one step at a time. Read Matthew 7:24–25.

I declare: "I know your deeds. See, I have placed before you an open door that no one can shut" (Revelation 3:8a, NIV).

AUGUST 9

No one can steal your happiness unless you give them the keys. The best prayer warriors are never angry. They know the one that angers you and controls you. They release them by pure forgiveness. And they pray for them. All stories are filled with brokenness, horrible choices, and great setbacks. They can also be filled with peace, grace, and major breakthroughs that saved your life, all orchestrated by the hand of God because of your faith. Choose your battles wisely. All the great setbacks made you a prayer warrior. As a warrior, you have learned to turn pain into power because you are here to make a difference. I have been built from every single mistake I have ever made. And so are you. Hate no one. Just because you took longer than others doesn't mean you have failed. Remember that. I changed from more godly wisdom. Declare: I am on the path of accomplishing my purpose for God's Kingdom. He calls me beautiful like it is my name. I am enough. A winner is just a loser that tried one more time. But the Lord is with me like a *mighty warrior*.

I declare: "I am on the path of accomplishing my purpose for God's Kingdom."

AUGUST 10

Strong people do not have attitudes; they have guidelines and goals. Look at your old life! Take a deep breath and declare, "I will never see you again." Become a priority in your own life. Take one step at a time towards what is right. Trust the Master of this universe, God; He has a bigger plan for you than you can ever completely understand. Hardcore focus will put you five years ahead in life. Do not underestimate the power of discipline and commitment. This life is full of lessons that have taught you the most and made you stronger. Declare: I am an overcomer of obstacles in my life. Life does not and will not come with a remote control. If you do not like something about your life, get going and change things. Own your story. Victory is around that corner. Stop stopping yourself. A bad attitude will ruin your own dream. Do it for you. Thirty years from now, no one will remember your choices but you. Discipline or regret? You will remember it. Only you. Boss up. When you know, you are hanging on by a thread... Make sure it is the hem of His garment. Prayer changes you and things. Nothing is impossible with God (Luke 1:37).

I declare: "I am an overcomer of obstacles in my life. Life does not and will not come with a remote control."

AUGUST 11

Joy-filled marriages do not just happen. It takes two willing people to build a foundation of love to stay happy. Smart people know what to say, but a godly, wise person knows whether to say it or not. Arguing with a fool will only prove that now there are two. When you stay healthy in your mind, you will not speak ill of others. Those who are truly happy people are usually kind to one another no matter what. Do not be just a good lawyer for yourself and make a very good judge for the mistakes of others. The softest pillow is having a clear conscience. Grades do not measure intelligence. Just like age does not measure maturity. I am a wooden spoon survivor. Spare the rod spoils the children. I was raised to treat the janitor and the CEO with the same respect. He will reward those who diligently seek Him. God is still at work even when we are not. Fools vent their anger, but the wise quietly hold it back. In everything, give thanks. You or I could not do this life one day without Jesus.

I declare:

The fear of the LORD is the beginning of wisdom; all who follow his precepts have good understanding. To him belongs eternal praise.

Psalm 111:10 (NIV)

AUGUST 12

I never really understood how heartbreak felt until I lost a few people that I loved in my life. And some walked away from me like it was the easiest thing in the world. That can crush a heart. Take charge of your emotions and declare out loud the promises of God. While others long to feel at home, they are not longing to be impressed. They are craving to feel like they are home. Create a space full of agape love so they come in, take off their shoes, and curl up with thankfulness and rest. It does not matter how small, how undone, how odd, or how old. Be known for your kindness. Influence your energy in the room filled with God's love. Fall in love with this process and the process of becoming the very best version of yourself. Be that person who turned their "cannot" into "cans" and their dreams into plans. No matter what! When we trust God with our broken dreams, we experience better dreams. Dream on. Rewards or regrets? God is not mocked. All seeds will eventually come into fruition. You will reap what you have planted (Galatians 6:7). Life is a process of sowing seeds. Your grateful attitude will bless you immediately.

I declare: "I will prove myself by purity, understanding, patience, and kindness, in the Holy Spirit and in sincere love (2 Corinthians 6:6)."

AUGUST 13

Are you struggling with negativity? Worrying about your future is not what God's best is for you. So, you must tell your mind to stop it. Now. Overthinking leads to negative thinking. Clearly, start meditating on positive thoughts immediately. Even scientists know the patterns of our brains change as we establish new patterns of thinking. Research backs up the practice of gratitude. Saying it out loud increases our happiness by 25 percent. Fix your mind, right now, on things that are good for you to think about, taking every thought captive. Read out loud Philippians 4:8. These daily practices will keep you in a positive "state of mind." Dance, love, sing, and live. Make gratitude a part of your daily routine. Declare: I am grateful for everything in my life! Start speaking, one at a time, out loud, each thing you are grateful for. Having a hard time feeling grateful when your heart is feeling heavy? If you cannot feel grateful for everything right now, be grateful for something. Start with naming a highlight of this new day. Decide that today will be amazing. Create your own happiness. You can keep waiting if you would like to. Or you can make it happen. Having gratitude will eliminate stress, shield you from negativity, rewire your brain, heal, improve sleep, boost your self-esteem, and improve relationships. Thankfulness has an amazing side effect. It increases your *joy!*

I declare: "I am grateful for everything in my life."

AUGUST 14

Your skin has a memory. In ten, twenty, and thirty years from this day, your skin will show the results of how you treated it. You are fearfully and wonderfully made by God. If my skin-care has a good routine, I must be mindful of a good routine with my God first, then my mate and my family. Also, include being good to myself on that list because I display myself every day for all my life. Let me make something very, very clear. Love the skin you are in. A beautiful or handsome you will require a commitment, not a miracle. Real men love Jesus. A wonderful life begins with exceptional care. Your life is an investment, not an expense. Happiness is a habit. Aging is a fact. A healthy life is not an overnight process or success. Work on you, for you. Be a student of God's love and grace. Always be learning. If you are going to quit anything: quit making excuses, quit wasting time, and quit being lifeless. This right here is a God-given lifestyle. There is no finish line. Declare: I do not have time for drama. Success is no accident. I am becoming the person I need to be for my mission on earth. The fruit of the Holy Spirit is love, joy, and peace. Remember, scriptures will not work unless you do. Plan on finishing the year God-strong. This is a good season to review your life and reflect on God's mercies.

I declare: "I am training for myself and my household. I am seeking God's purpose for my life."

AUGUST 15

People cannot see faith. And they cannot see God. They only can see how you handle all the bad situations in your life with God and your faith. You matter. Your existence means you are worthy. Do not let other people tell you who you are. Are you ready for a new chapter in your life? Declare: I am enough. I have always been enough. I will always be enough. Today, I will not stress over things I cannot control. Nothing changes if nothing changes. Success begins with the moment you start trying. Every accomplishment starts with your decision to try. You get what you work for, not what you wish for. You only need someone to accept you completely. What you think about yourself is way more important than what others think about you. Stand in faith, even when you are having the hardest time of your life. Work in silence and let your success speak for itself. You only fail if you quit. If all you can do is crawl, start crawling. God can restore what is broken and change it all into amazing. All you need is Him and faith. A simple prayer, "Jesus, keep me in Your presence," will keep your mind untangled. His spirit will protect your mind, body, and soul.

I declare: "I am enough. I have always been enough. I will always be enough."

AUGUST 16

It is okay. You just forgot who you are and who you belong to. Welcome back. You are amazing. I cannot wait to see what God has in store for you. Nothing in life is more important than your family. Give them time. A person who truly values you would not ever put themselves in a position to lose you. But blessed is the one who trusts in the Lord and whose confidence is in Him (Jeremiah 17:7). The things you take for granted someone else is praying for. Love beyond words. Where there is agape love, there are always miracles. He rescues those whose spirits are crushed. "Sometimes" is "now." Happy relationships stay beautiful when the people involved are good forgivers. Do not spoil what you have right now by desiring what you have not. There is no way to be perfect, but a million ways to be kind. A truly rich family is one whose children run into their arms when their hands are empty.

I declare: "For where your treasure is, there your heart will also be."

AUGUST 17

If today were your last day, would you be living life the way you do? Or would you be more mindful and more intentional about yourself and others? Would you reach out in forgiveness more? Would you show more love? More patience? The purpose of this life is to be more useful, more kind, more understanding, and more compassionate. Others may feel your attitude, so they will not listen to your words. Your attitude is just like a price tag. It shows others your value and, seriously, what you really think of yourself. Step into a room, and your energy will introduce you before you open your mouth. Do you know what healthy self means? Heal thy self, of course, with the help of the Holy Spirit and His God spells, which is the Word of God. Then that healthy mind will not speak ill of others or thy self. Before you speak, think how you would feel if someone spoke it to you. Even if you are mad, think before you talk. Words may be forgiven but not forgotten. Our tongues have no bones, but they certainly can break a heart. Key: You always do your best when you feel your best. Hint: Take care first thing of the day: your mind, body, and soul. Keep fighting for what you want to be daily. The work God does in the darkness is preparing you for the awesomeness on the other side of it.

I declare: "I will keep a healthy mind, body, and spirit by the words I speak, starting first thing every morning."

AUGUST 18

Absolutely, you are free to choose. But you will not be free from good or bad consequences of the choice you made. Remember that! Words will mean nothing when your actions are the very opposite. And why do we get upset at someone for being who they have always been? Happiness is a choice. Kindness is a choice. Being positive is a choice. Respect is a choice. And you will pick what you plant. How you live, you will end up with. Ignoring the red flags is a great way to end up at the wrong destination. Your actions are free; it is how you decide to use them that may cost you. You always have a choice. Always. Every day is a second chance. Decide. Commit. Succeed. Do. It. Now. You are not done. You are not stuck. It is not over for you. What lies ahead of you is far greater than you can ever imagine. All things work together for good for those who keep their trust in God (Romans 8:28).

I declare: "The Lord will fight for you; you need only to be still."

AUGUST 19

Faith is like marriage. You cannot cheat on it and expect it to work. Be your inspiration. First, others will make fun of you. Then, they will ask how you got through it. Sweat off the stress. When I lost all my excuses, I found a routine that became golden to my mind, body, and soul man. Clear your mind of, "I cannot do this now." Excuses are useless. It becomes something you just cannot live without. The more you work on it, the easier it is to pray, kneeling down. I believe that when the mind is strong, the body thinks less of the flesh. What seems impossible today becomes possible for God (Mark 10:27). Now, your faith test is just a warm-up. You will never know your limits unless you push yourself through them. If you have time for social media, you have time for seeking the Lord. You are only one decision away from a good mood. Push yourself because no one else is going to do it for you. Fall in love with taking care of your mind, body, and soul. I like who I am becoming. Do not dare to complain. Fear of faith will either create you or destroy you. You choose.

I declare: "Relieve the troubles of my heart and free me from my anguish."

AUGUST 20

When you find a routine that is good for you, it is like gold. A lack of boundaries invites a lack of respect. Be strong enough to forgive without receiving an apology. Pay attention because everything is a teacher. One thing I do know for sure is that God is a way-maker. He will make the way to get things done. He will fix it or shift it or turn it around. I know exactly what you are thinking; there seems no way? I can rest in the fact that God is in control. Which means... you can be sure things are out of your control, and you are not to act out of control. For the eyes of the Lord run to and from throughout the earth, to show Himself strong on the behalf of those whose hearts are loyal to Him (2 Chronicles 16:19). I have read the final chapter, and God wins. You are being pushed out of your comfort zone, but you can walk in bravery knowing that greater is He that is in you than he that is in this world. Do not panic.

God is there right with you. After all, He is the *King* of the universe. Look to the Lord and His strength; seek His face always.

I declare: "Many are the plans in a person's heart, but it is the Lord's purpose that prevails."

AUGUST 21

Say, "I have got what it takes." You were custom designed for your life. No matter what anyone thinks! If God is for you, it does not matter who is against you. Your spirit will heal with joy. I believe in the power of love. Recognize that your unique life matters. No one will ever make a difference being like anyone else. To be successful, you will not have to prove anything to anyone. Just be you, and the right situations and people will find you. You must have the courage to be disliked. And patience is when you are supposed to be upset, but you choose to understand. The most powerful thing you can do right now is to be patient while things are falling into place. Silence is a true friend. Overthinking is what will stop you. Words are like keys; if you choose them right, they can open any heart and shut any mouth. Let the silence do the talking. Actions from others are never about you. Do not act on negativity. Detach from it. Your taste in people will change when you learn to love yourself. Let my steps stay on your tracks so that my feet will not stumble (Psalm 17:15). God will carry you. Walk in love. The battle is not ours but God's. Your growth may scare you sometimes, but do not stop. Instead of overthinking, try overloving.

I declare: "Better is the end of a thing than the beginning of it, and the patient in spirit is better than the proud in spirit."

AUGUST 22

The story that will most change your life is the one you live. It is the most honest, most human book you have inside your soul. Writing is one of the only things I feel I should be doing! It is creating something that has never existed. Write your story! Be kind even on your bad days. Hate is heavy; let it go. Have faith in who you were created to be. Make it your goal to lead a quiet life. Pray first, then make plans. Do not vent to others. Write it down. Pray over it. Then throw it away. Tell God and keep it to yourself. Sometimes when we get overwhelmed, we forget how big God is. God listens, and He understands. Pray on it. Pray over it. Most of all, pray until you get through it. Do not get poisoned by stress, pressure, and frustration. Never stop praying. I love Jesus because, in our crazy world, He is my *peace*, my King. God is mercy. And it is bigger than anything you are going through. Fix your eyes on Jesus, the author and perfecter of our faith.

I declare: "Now may the Lord of peace Himself always give me peace in every way."

AUGUST 23

When you feel tired, it is not because you have done too much. It is because you have done so little of what sparks the light inside of you. In school, you are given the lesson, then the test. In this life, you get the test, then the lesson. I found a way to shift my poor thinking. My morning routine includes ten minutes of speaking positive affirmations over myself. And I laugh when I think my childhood punishments became some of my best adult goals. Go to sleep early. Rise up early. And read faith-filled books. Pray and speak to the Lord, all on purpose. The day you plant the seed is not the day you eat the fruit. Lord bless my hustle and reduce my stress. No matter how difficult your past is, your future is still spotless. You change the world by your example and the seeds you plant. Your mind is your weapon. Your mindset is what will separate you for the good. Every next level of life will always demand a different commitment from you. Work on the person you want to have in your life. It is on. Self-care? Is taking your power back. You were designed to live the life you are living. The door that just swung open is not for you to run through or run away. It is for your new direction, discovery, and discipline. You were prepared for this.

I declare: "I am not rash with my mouth, and my heart is not hasty to utter words before God."

AUGUST 24

Ask the Holy Spirit to fill you daily so that nothing of the flesh can stick to you and drag you down. Stay in tune to your own purpose and place. Positive position is so important for the next move in your life. Stop falling for emotional tricks; they are ordered distractions by the enemy to get you discouraged about life, so you forget your focus. I know you were designed for the more. It is up to you to stay strong and do the hard work. Nothing worth anything comes easy. You must push yourself daily, especially against the emotions of what others say and do to you. Safeguard yourself with the Word. It is so important in the Kingdom World not to stay stuck in the flesh. It is deadly for your spiritual growth. You can speak in tongues, you can quote scripture, and you can go to church and listen to your favorite preacher. But none of this will work if you are not obedient to your calling. Put aside the weight that comes against you and rise above it all. Work on your spiritual maturity! You may have to shut down for spiritual maintenance. But that is necessary where God is about to take you. Can I hear a hallelujah and an amen? If God is for you, no man can fool you. Be prepared, daily, to walk out your mission that Christ has laid before you. Walk in the Word.

I declare: "I think about sticking with things because the thoughts of the diligent tend only to plenty, but everyone who is impatient and hasty hastens only to want."

AUGUST 25

Watch out for blind spots. Anger, resentment, hurt, and frustration can and will stop the flow of the Holy Spirit. Rise above it! Focus on becoming so involved in your own growth that you forget something bad even happened. Stop pulling open all the flowers. They must bloom according to His plan. Wake up every morning and say out loud, "I can do all things through Christ who strengthens me" (Philippians 4:13, NKJV). Mirrors lie; they do not show you what is inside. Grief is the price of love. Your first thought of the day should be, "Thank you." When you focus on how good the good is, the good gets better. Your most beautiful attire is your smile. Be someone who puts the phone down to listen to others. Do not speak poorly of others. When you can listen to others' ideas or feelings without anger or frustration, you give them a wonderful gift. You make it safe for others to express themselves. A passion for God is the most attractive feature you can possess. I just want to be thankful for being a reason for someone to forward to the next day. When someone can handle your flaws, love you on moody days, and kiss you when you do not look so great, they are worth it. There is no fear in love. Perfect love drives out fear. Loving others through hard times and valleys reveals the Gospel of Christ in our lives.

I declare: "My God will liberally supply (fill to the full) my every need according to His riches in glory in Christ Jesus."

AUGUST 26

The most unhealthy relationships share a common interest, a lack of trust. Trust is the foundation everything is built on. Communication is another key. Also, throw in a combination of respect, friendship, understanding, and forgiveness. If most of your arguments stay soft, most likely, you will keep stable relationships. Uplift as many people in a day that you can. Spread the spirit of joy. Show support even if it goes against your own opinion. Your problems should be considered team problems. Loving relationships are not magic; they are intentional by choice. Find the cause of the things that trigger you. Pray about them and release them. Once you know triggers, you can begin the work needed for emotional freedom. There is so much power in prayer. Your happiness does not depend on others; it depends on your inner self. Replace sorry with thank you. Instead of, "Sorry I am late," say, "Thank you for waiting on me." Edit yourself frequently; you are a masterpiece created by the Master of the universe, our God! Make connections, be that bridge in people's relationships with others. I love helping people connect. Build bridges today.

I declare: "I am learning how to be content (satisfied to the point where I am not disturbed or disquieted) in whatever state I am."

AUGUST 27

Self-care is taking back your power. Start eating food without labels, and you will no longer need to count calories. Exercise is the most underutilized antidepressant. Food is the most abused anxiety drug. Symptoms are not your enemy. Fall in love with taking care of yourself, spirit, mind, and body. What you put at the end of your fork is more powerful than anything you will ever find in a drugstore. Let's pay the farmer, not the drugstore. Sunshine. Water. Rest. Fresh air. Diet. Exercise. I cannot control anything in life except what I choose to eat or not eat. Our bodies were not meant to deal with fake foods. If it is a plant-based food, eat it. If it is made in a plant, do not. Eating organic is not a trend. It has been around for a long time. If you do not take care of your body, who will? Seek God and pray first thing daily. Tell yourself you are beautiful or handsome daily. Read faith-filled messages daily. Start doing planks and challenge yourself. We grow old because we just stop. Why should we be concerned about what others think of us? Do we have more confidence in their opinions than we do in our own? Do you trust Him? God can do it just like that! God is the best doctor. Your personal prayer is the best medicine. Once upon a time, all food was organic.

I declare: "I am raised up for this very purpose, that I might display His power in my life, and that His name will be proclaimed in all the Earth."

A U G U S T   2 8

Win the battle for your mind. As a mighty weapon, decisions and choices guide life. Our words and actions begin with a thought. What you will wear, your attitude, and what you will eat or drink all begin with a thought! A prayerful anointing. You are blessed because you believe the Lord will do what He said He would do. I need the Lord in every single moment of my life. If you are praying about it, God is working on it. Worry means you are trying to figure everything out yourself. Do not stay in the boat when God is calling you to walk on the water. If it is hard for you to pray right now, it is a trick of the enemy! That liar knows your praying will limit him. Only one book can transform your life, the Bible. It is the only book whose author is always present when one reads it. How powerful is that! If you think God has been silent, then your Bible has been closed. Stay hungry for His Word; it is life-changing. Live carefully; your actions may be the only Bible some people read. The Holy Spirit never enters a man and lets him live like the world does. It is so powerful and life-changing. He will qualify you to do what He has called you to do. Devil says, "They are all mine." Jesus responds so confidently, "Over my dead body." No matter what the enemy does, he is defeated. Rejoice! You have the victory.

I declare: "Christ is seated in heavenly places, and I am seated in Him."

AUGUST 29

It is time. Lay aside every snare, every trap, every toxic thought, every damaging word, and realize they are from the devil. Why? Because he knows how powerful you are to the Kingdom of God. Watch and pray for God to order your footsteps and lay aside the weight of old problems. They were sent to you to stop the plan that God has ordained over you before you were put in your mother's womb. And remember this: *Nothing* can stop the amazing plan from God over you. Nothing but your choices. Get up. Do not quit. Open the Word. Decree, out loud, aggressively, the promises of God. That will get the devil out of your life. Be humble in life, but spiritually, you need to be aggressive. Work the Word. There is power in the Word of God. It is time. Move on and walk in your anointing. There is someone out there that needs to hear your testimony. Fear cannot stay. Doubt must fall. Procrastination must flee. In Jesus' name. Decide and declare, "I am more than a conqueror. I have the victory. I am blessed and highly favored by the King of kings. Hallelujah."

Forgiveness is a must to move on. It is not just about you. It is about living life abundantly. For you and your whole family. A problem is not just yours; it touches the whole family.

I declare: "I am more than a conqueror."

AUGUST 30

You have been delivered from evil, do not keep in touch. Something you prayed about is ready to happen. Seek God for your answer; He will show you what you need. Those broken pieces? God is fixing them. Everything is going to be okay. Repeat that out loud. Your relationship should mean that you come to help each other to be better. Believe in one another. Support and build up one another. Be their peace and not their problem. Some days one may struggle, but you pick it up and be the eighty/twenty because they may need you. That is unconditional love. There will be smiles, tears, attitudes, and discussions in every relationship. Difference does not separate people; silence does. You are a team. In life, you are in control of your attitude and your effort. Do not judge someone because they sin differently than you. We are all sinners saved by God's grace. Put away toxic talk and treat others the way you want to be treated. This is the way of God. Stop fueling the drama. Negativity is a dead spirit. So is complaining, and it is draining to you and others around you. It is not just about you. Everyone in life is important, everyone. Try something different. Try building up. Try complementing. Try encouraging. Try just keeping quiet. Good things are being released from heaven; get ready to receive. Beauty for ashes.

I declare: "God loves those who love Him, and those who seek Him early and diligently shall find Him."

AUGUST 31

News flash: You cannot control anything. Shift to what you can believe in, your faith. No room for people who try to make you feel small or insecure. You need folks who inspire you and build you up. If you do not like something, take away its only power, your attention. You cannot rush God's timing. An ending is not rejection; it is God's way of promoting you to a new season. God is always fighting for you. Focus on God, not the storm. God-confidence. There is a kind of love that God only knows. You can overcome that addiction, that bad relationship, that bend in the road, or that sickness. Tell that mountain about how big your God is. The maker of heaven and earth. Anyone that kneels before God daily can stand before anyone. He has a name for every star. There are days I must give it all to God and go to bed. Put your hope right now in God. Prayer is a life changer. Commit yourself. I will not be shaken. Cultivate kindness. Focus on the Lord. Be bold. Be brave. Be courageous.

I declare: "I am enough."

September

*Let your conversation be always full of grace, seasoned with
salt, so that you may know how to answer everyone.*

Colossians 4:6 (NIV)

Your words are powerful. Be careful what you speak.

SEPTEMBER 1

When others talk about or against you, just laugh. That will not stop God from blessing you. I am that crazy person that believes God can and will do anything. I love it! It just makes my faith *soar*. Get excited. The name of Jesus is above all other names (Philippians 2:9). And believe His Word. If God is for you, who can be against you? No weapon formed against me or my household shall prosper in the mighty name of Jesus (Isaiah 54:17). Just when you need Him, Jesus is nearby. Have hope. Do not lose heart. Get unbelief out of the way.

You have a hidden power inside of you; it is the Holy Spirit. Get ready. Declare the Word out loud over your situation. And be careful not to listen to others who do not have a prayer life. Do not get locked in unforgiveness. It is a designed trick from the enemy to keep you stuck. He whom the Son sets free is free indeed. Remember, the devil has no new tricks. Be aware. Stay awesome in what God says you can do. Walk by faith. Trust the Lord. Praise Him right now for what He is doing for you in that situation that looks dead. There is life and power in the Word of God. Disappointment stops hope. But with God, hope is always there. Walk through that door of hope today. The best relationships, the best marriage, the best results, the best opportunities, and the best life is for you with God!

I declare the word out loud over my situations. I will not listen to others who do not have a prayer life.

SEPTEMBER 2

Negative people speak problems over solutions that God spoke to you in prayer. Jehovah Jireh means the Lord will provide what He has promised you. Non-forgiveness is too much past pain and not enough good presence of your new season. Who can stop the Lord almighty? What He opens, no one can close. What He closes, no one can open. That is the Word of God. *Powerful.* Change for you, no one else. Have you been praying, and still no answer? Have you hoped things would change by now? Do not forget the things He has already done. Hope. You have just not seen it. There is no greater gift to give someone than the gift of your time. Listen without fixing or changing. He is moving; good things are coming. Just believe it. The devil does not come after one in darkness; he comes after you when you are trying to get out. Reread. It is up to you to break generational curses. State, "This curse right here is where it runs out with me, in Jesus' name." It stops here, now. God can and will turn your life around. He did it for me. Success is commitment. Start by reading one page in your Bible, praying on your knees for one minute, walking one lap, writing one paragraph, drinking one cup of water, listening to one faith-filled sermon, and encouraging one person. *Start* today. *Repeat* tomorrow.

I declare: "Through faith in Him, my hope will continue to grow by the power of the Holy Spirit."

SEPTEMBER 3

This is what poisons relationships, hidden resentment.

Graciously, say if something bothers you. Watch your words: they are containers that carry faith or fear, love or hate, encouragement or correction, and acceptance or rejection. Positive people do have negative thoughts; they just do not let those thoughts haunt or control them. Release anger for your own well-being. Harboring anger creates disease. If you cannot act kind, stay quiet. "I praise You, God, for I am fearfully and wonderfully made." Leap out in faith, trust God, and do the right thing. Be mindful of others' feelings, not just your own. It is about your purpose in life to help others and not be paid back for the good you have done. God is the one who will bless you. When He blesses you, it will be worth much more than what anyone can ever possibly do. He rewards those who trust Him and always do the right thing. Ask yourself to get out of the way. Let go of overthinking. Be rock solid at your core but stay calm. The best people embrace both. Life is not for your agenda. It is for God's purpose to work through you to bless other people. The more time you spend thinking about the Word, the more ability you will have to help others out.

I declare: "When I give to the needy, I do not let my left hand know what my right hand is doing so that my giving may be in secret. Then my Father, who sees what is done in secret, will reward me."

SEPTEMBER 4

You cannot seek your own way! Sometimes, you may lose yourself, but that is okay. It is all a part of our journey throughout life. Make sure your comeback is way stronger than your setback. All you can change is you. Your foundation should be built on God's love and self-love. Now you can embrace others that are different than you. Wake up every morning expecting to be better than you were yesterday. Keep that past under your feet and the blood of Jesus. Love yourself so much that when someone does treat you wrong, you will recognize it immediately. Pray for them. Rise above it. Let it go. It is God's agenda you are living. Do not get worked up. You are too amazing not to feel good about yourself. Someone's opinion of you is really their opinion of themselves. Remember that! Grateful instead of complaining. Take care of yourself; that is your power. There is no limit to how radiant, alive, energetic, motivated, and positive you can be. It is so empowering; it is not emotional. It is powerful. Create a life you love. It is all up to you. You are responsible for how you act, respond, think, talk, and live, no matter what. It is no one else's fault! Your life is your life. What you think, you become. I do not look for happiness because it is already within me. It is when you leave God's will, you will "live" a hard time.

I declare: "This is my comfort and consolation in my affliction: that Your word has revived me and given me life."

SEPTEMBER 5

If you want to begin your day positively, then work on having a positive mindset. Be mindful of others and what you speak to them; this is a huge start. If you are feeling critical, angry, or want to convey a wrong impression, then pray about what you shall speak before you open your mouth and ruin your whole day. Fear has no grip on you. Shake it off. No negative self-talk is allowed either. Fall in love with taking care of your mind, body, and soul. Improve your prayer life. Real men have strong faith. I always thank God for giving me another chance. Do not worry about what people say behind your back because God is going to bless you right in front of them. Something is happening that you cannot see; God is building your foundation stronger. Your life will only get better when you seek God first. God uses everything. He is very creative. My prayer for you today is for God to pour a fresh anointing on you and your family. God is sending the right people in your pathway. God breaks chains, not promises. The words you speak become the house you live in. God gave us amazing minds. Choose being joyful no matter what.

I declare: "I have been anointed by the Holy One, and I know (the truth)."

SEPTEMBER 6

Do not be afraid to grow. End those bad habits. Know your worth. There are times when my greatest accomplishment is just keeping my mouth shut. This helps overcome something you are dealing with. Zip it. God is using your experience to develop your character to match your calling. When we pray for each other, something supernatural takes place. Take a moment right now and pray for that person or that situation. Stop worrying about how it is going to happen and start trusting God that it will. Fear is a liar. Believe it will happen. A smile is understood in every single language. Keep smiling. Stay in prayer; your answer is closer than you think. Let others judge you. Let them gossip. Your job is to stay kind and keep smiling. Others' opinions are their problems, not yours. Isn't that freeing? Everyone is entitled to their opinion. You are the finest, most beautiful person ever. Crush your goals. If all the words you spoke yesterday appeared on your skin, would you still be beautiful or handsome? God has given you the spirit to be able to do amazing things for yourself and others. Champions win. Losers complain. You are a person with purpose. Focus on living a positive life. With God's

I declare: "I am honoring God in everything I do. I am qualified by God to do it. Done."

SEPTEMBER 7

Manipulating and forcing an outcome is not from God. It is evil. All things work together for good for those who love God and who are called according to His purpose. Do not judge. The devil wants you to worry, so be careful who you listen to. Let the Lord fight your battles. He has not lost one yet. Start calling yourself: healed, whole, happy, blessed, and mighty. Stop trying to change others and their life. Keep your eyes on you, and work on you. It is not a good idea to pick up something God helped you put away. Quit stopping yourself. God does not check your bank account; he is checking your faith. Work more on your faith. You may feel drained emotionally and physically. God will see you through. Rest in the fact that God is in control. You are not a failure. Declare: I will not drive myself crazy over-thinking. I will trust God for the path I am on and enjoy this moment with gratitude. We will have hard days. We will feel disappointed. We all face challenges. But the real beauty in life is completely accepting ourselves and knowing that I am more than a conqueror and I am not giving up.

I declare: "I will not drive myself crazy overthinking. I will trust God for the path I am on and enjoy this moment with gratitude."

SEPTEMBER 8

Your problems are not stop signs. Look at them as guidelines. You have got to learn how to say no without feeling guilty. Those boundaries are healthy to your soul. Respect and care for yourself. I am sure, like most of us, our stories are filled with broken promises, horrible choices, and ugly truths. But I do know for sure firsthand your comeback has been so filled with major peace, joy, and God's grace, which has saved your life and mine! If nothing else, most people have taught you how not to be. The Holy Spirit will show you how to heal thyself. Your challenge, like mine, is to silence the mind from overthinking. Learning to ignore negativity is one of the greatest paths to your inner peace. Accept your flaws and go to work on being a better you. If you do, then no one can use them against you. It is time to regain your balance. Watch your thoughts, for they become your words. Do not let your mind be more talkative than your mouth. Count your blessings; it will turn your life around. Pray first before you make any plans or changes. If you do not come from a loving family, a loving family must come from you. Claim it in Jesus' name. Being in love is not a mood; it is a commitment. If you want to be trusted, just be honest. Vengeance is the Lord's.

I declare: "I am very, very careful never to compromise with the people around me, and I do not follow their evil ways."

SEPTEMBER 9

What situation has you tied up today? Spend some time today meditating on God's Word. Your focus should be on Him. Deal with others' flaws as gently as you do your own. Admire without jealousy. Most people struggle with liking themselves. And are you still worried about who does not like you? Life is a puzzle. Happiness will start with your own thinking. You do not need a reason to be grateful. Check your pulse. Faith in God will change everything for everyone. The number one skill in this life is to never quit learning. Give yourself credit for those days you made it when you thought you could not. Do not trust fear; it does not know your real strength. Encourage instead of complaining. The kinder you are, the more beautiful you become. Declare: I can be kind to myself. I can accept myself. I am joyful and excited about today.

You are God's masterpiece (Ephesians 2:10). You are going to make it. Trust God (Psalm 23). For with God, nothing is impossible (Luke 1:37). I am looking forward to this day. I have the power within me to make it a great day. I offer my best self today. Begin with God this moment. Your mind? Keep it fixed on God, your first priority of each day.

I declare: "I can be kind to myself. I can accept myself. I am joyful and excited about today."

SEPTEMBER 10

You are not just doing it for yourself. Your transformation will help and inspire others. You will not succeed if you only work on your goals on the days you feel like it. *Believing* is the only way to achieve. Here is how it all happens...One step at a time. *Secret?* There is no secret. You have got to do the seeking, praying, and working. This journey is all up to you. If you stop, you are only stopping yourself. I am allergic to negativity and negative people. What God is preparing you for is worth the wait. How does it all work? The foundation of truth! Declare: I will help you speak and teach you what to say (Exodus 4:12). Be strong and courageous; the Lord is with you (Joshua 1:9). "Lord, renew my energy" (Psalm 103:5). "I have called you by your name; you are Mine" (Isaiah 43:1b, NKJV). You were born for such a time as this (Esther 4:14). You must start to be great. Decluttering is self-care. You see, being organized is not about being perfect; it is about getting your whole world to work for you. Get unstuck.

I declare: "I will help you speak and teach you what to say."

SEPTEMBER 11

He healed the one who arrested Him, served the one who betrayed Him, and loved this world. God is up to something, or the devil would not be fighting us so hard. The best revenge is not to be like your enemy. Your growth will be uncomfortable because you have never been here before. Forgive others quickly; you do not need to sit in the seat of the scornful. Love them anyway (Luke 23:34). And it is not your job to like me; it is mine. The most important decision you will make today is what you will not say. God will provide. You lack nothing. Use what God has already given you. The devil will tell you constantly to look at your sin. But God says, "Look at my Son." Whatever you are not changing, you are choosing. Changes are wonderful. He loved you at your darkest (Romans 5:8). The serpent did not tempt Adam and Eve to steal, kill, or destroy; he simply tempted them to question the Word of God. Never speak words that will allow the enemy to think he is winning and winning you over. Be careful what you are speaking. Be that someone who makes everyone feel good, not just your own family but others who are different than you. That is agape love.

I declare: "When I walk in love, God is present."

S E P T E M B E R   1 2

And yet, after all, that life has blessed me. I certainly know one thing for sure; I would be ruined, rotten, and torn if it were not for me seeking God first daily. I do not want to make anyone feel short of anything or put a guilt trip on you, but you must set apart some time in your day just for you and the Lord. I, personally, need to seek Him first thing when I wake up. I cannot start my day without it. Success in anything just does not happen. You must "make it happen." Beauty does not rinse off. Do not forget when your plans are committed to the Lord, your plans will succeed. We know that in all things, God works for the good of those who love Him (Romans 8:28). He can break every chain. Declare: I am confident because I can admit who I am. I am a child of the living God. I have chosen to be happy because it is good for my health. God will speak if you take the time to listen, and He will listen to you when you take the quiet time to pray. Your character counts.

I declare: "I am confident because I can admit who I am."

SEPTEMBER 13

You cannot use an egg unless it's broken. The Lord is near to the broken-hearted and saves those who are crushed in spirit (Psalm 34:18). Your most powerful prayer is, "Change me." The best way to heal your broken heart is to be sure you give God all the pieces. The one who guards his mouth protects his life. The one who opens his lips invites in his own spoil (Proverbs 13:3). I am not lucky. You do not know how much I pray, read faith-filled books, listen to faith-filled sermons, and devote my time to seeking the Lord. I am blessed by God. When the Holy Spirit enters a man, he cannot remain the same. Blaming keeps that wound open. Let it go. Forgiveness heals.

You are most like the Lord when you remain silent under attack. The struggle is real. But so is God. I found my life when I laid it down. When God wants you to grow, He will make you very uncomfortable. Love them anyway (Luke 23:34). Key? Empty you of yourself. Let God fill you with the Holy Spirit. Ask. Love your enemies, do good to those who hate you, bless those who curse you, and pray for those who have mistreated you (Luke 6:27–28). You worry too much! Remember, God's got this. Love does not dishonor (1 Corinthians 13:5)! Prayer is your weapon. But you shall receive power when the Holy Spirit has come upon you (Acts 1:8).

I declare: "If I forgive people their trespasses, my heavenly Father will also forgive me."

SEPTEMBER 14

Help others remove the specks as you choose to love others for who they are and what they are going through. Judging is a lovely way to distract you from what is wrong with you. Do not judge, or you, too, will be judged. For in the same way you judge, you, too, will be judged (Matthew 7:1). Learn to live in a place of resting peace. Deal with problems together. There is no need to panic. "The name of the Lord is a strong tower; the righteous run to it and are safe" (Proverbs 18:10, NKJV). Your breath of life is an amazing gift. Your physical life is a beautiful blessing. But your *spiritual* life is the diamond. You are a treasure to God. And diamonds must be tested and tried for their beauty to shine. How do you view life? Are you the solution or the problem? Do whatever it takes to refresh your steps. Give yourself a break, do not become preoccupied with judging. It is a trick from the enemy. It is a trap to ensnare you to get stuck and stop the flow of the Holy Spirit. "Blessed are those who have learned to acclaim You, Lord" (Psalm 89:15). Your life on earth will be a challenge, just like mine. As seasons change, ask the Lord to change you too. Do not be too quick to judge God; He may be doing the work you cannot see to protect you from something.

I declare: "I submit myself to God, I resist the devil, and he must flee."

SEPTEMBER 15

Your strongest muscle and worst enemy is your mind.

Train it well, renew it daily. Beautiful faces are plenty, but beautiful hearts are scarce. When you start to carry your own water, you learn the value of every drop. Your mind is powerful. Thoughts create, destroy, and experience all things. God has given us all power over evil. Strengthen your mind, read the Word. If faith comes by hearing, then what and who are you listening to? Whatever you desire, when you pray, *believe* that you receive it, and you shall have it by faith (Mark 11:24). The Holy Spirit changes you from the inside out. You have the power to change toxic thoughts. Change the way you live your life, stay filled with joy, peace, hope, and power from God. Daily renew your heart and soul, no different than day-to-day functions such as brushing your teeth. They are all vital to living your best life. Any thoughts about you today? Whatever they are, your feet and life will follow. It will destroy you or lead you to your God-given destiny. Train your brain to think continually on things that are true, honorable, worthy of respect, right, pure, wholesome, lovely, admirable, excellent, worthy of praise, and peaceful. Keep these on your mind and implant them in your heart (Philippians 4:8). Decide to pray instead of worry. It begins with you.

I declare: "I desire to live in peak happiness, thinking and speaking."

SEPTEMBER 16

Always be the type of person you would like to meet.

Our world needs who you were created to be. Yesterday was very heavy; stop carrying it around. Put it down. Work on you, for you. Scared? Great! You will not grow by staying in that comfort zone. Terrified of what is next? You are finally on the right track. If plan A did not work, remember that the alphabet has twenty-five more letters. Never stop being a fantastic person. Rumors are carried by worldly people. It is okay; let it all go. You only get to change and work on you anyways. A strong person knows that they have the potential to really shine for this world. Your true strength lies in your ability to lay down your life so that God can work through you and shine. The enemy does not want your stuff: he wants your mind, your attitude, your heart, and your faith. Never assume quiet is weak. Have three goals to improve: your health, your spiritual growth, and your mind. Worry is worshiping your problems. Have a plan and a prayer. "[...] I have heard your prayer and seen your tears; I will heal you... (2 Kings 20:5, NIV)

I declare: "I have faith in the unseen."

SEPTEMBER 17

Let who think whatever. Let them judge you. Do not let hard days win. Stop fighting battles with others who are at war with themselves. This is your life. Do not worry about what others do. Self-love is a must. Everybody is not your God-given assignment. That is why you are drained. Pray for people who respond nastily and stay upset over the simple things. It has nothing to do with you. There is so much I would like to say, but nah, it is just not worth losing my peace over and stopping the overflow of the Holy Spirit. Your future needs you. Your past does not. Shut the door. Handle your business. And do not let everyone know about it. Love the experience; this is your teacher. Let it go. Change the channel. Turn it off. Mute. Breathe.

I declare: "When I am trying to please God, He makes even my worst enemies be at peace with me."

SEPTEMBER 18

Do not listen to what people say! Watch what they do first! Be patient; everything will come together. The Holy Spirit will help you pray (Romans 8:26–27). Pray. Set goals. Work hard. Thank God. Stay humble. Say daily, "The healing power of God is working in me right now. Every day, I get better and better in every way." Wake up with praise. No power in hell, no scheme of man could ever pluck me from God's plan (Romans 8:39). "'I will restore you to health and heal your wounds,' declares the Lord" (Jeremiah 30:17a, NIV). "You will receive power when the Holy Spirit comes upon you..." (Acts 1:8a, NIV)

Satan cannot read our thoughts, but he can hear our words. What are you speaking? Praise God out loud. Turn your car into a war room of prayer. I declare increase of joy, love, happiness, and healing to enter my life. I release all fear, doubt, negativity, and unforgiveness that is blocking my blessing. My increase begins now!

I declare: "I listen to and obey God's voice. He will be my God, and I will be one of His people."

SEPTEMBER 19

Happiness shows up when I stop complaining about the troubles I see. Becoming strong will not start in the gym. It always starts in your head. God is still writing my story. Have you found someone who is willing to struggle with you just so they can build with you? That is *love*. You will find no greater wealth in this world than peace of mind. A million likes will never be enough if you do not like yourself. If you do not make time for your own wellness, you will be forced to make time for your illness. Read that again. If you put healing words in your head, your body will listen. Your brain listens to the command of your own voice. Powerful. You are not responsible for anyone else's happiness, and you never were. Set yourself free. Unconditional happiness is not a fairy tale. It is a state of mind. My alone time is sacred. Be a light for all to see (Matthew 5:16).

I declare: "He who guards his mouth keeps his life. But he who opens wide, his lips come to ruin."

SEPTEMBER 20

Knowledge is not enough; you must apply. Willing is not enough either; we must do what is right, especially when no one is looking. You are what you do when you are alone. Doing right makes your pathway clear, or you will never see the full path. The most important thing is to do the right thing. Satan fools the mind, the thoughts, and the soul with things that can cloud your view. Spiritual maturity includes morals and respect for others' goods. Spiritual maturity is not measured by how much you praise or how much you know; it is measured by how straight you walk in obedience. It is being more God-conscious. If it costs your peace, it is way too expensive. Spiritual maturity will never exceed our knowledge of the Bible. To know it is one thing. To do it is another thing. Be the best version of yourself. Live so that when your children see fairness and integrity, they think of you. People look at the outward appearance, but the Lord looks at the heart (1 Samuel 16:17).

I declare: "I seek You, and I am found by You."

SEPTEMBER 21

Remove the dead weight in your mind; one by one, pluck them out and lay them at the feet of God. God is dealing with our character this new season so we can recognize others that are not spending time with Him. We need to safeguard ourselves through prayer. He wants us to stay in forgiveness and pray for those who have used us to keep perfect peace with others who do not follow the power of the Holy Spirit. God is revealing His character to us. We need to ask the Holy Spirit daily to be filled with His power and to order our steps. Lay aside every weight that will pull you down: gossip, unfairness, fear, doubt, slander, and finger-pointing. They are all straight from hell to stop the flow of the Holy Spirit. Encourage yourself. And check your own heart. God is moving fast, and you do not want to miss this next season of operating in His beautiful character. If you are serious, He will show you what the next step is. I am serious about changing me from the inside out. It will take twenty-one days to lay it all out before the Lord and do a total detox in your heart. Get excited to see what the Lord is about to do (Romans 12:2). Do not be conformed to this world but be transformed by renewing your mind.

I declare: "I call out to High God, the God who holds me together. He sends orders from heaven and saves me. God delivers generous love. He makes good on His word."

SEPTEMBER 22

In this life, there will always be someone who will need your forgiveness. Especially if you suffer with perfection and performance. Take the focus off yourself. Put down those emotions too. Release them to God. Do not compare; that is the worst thing. Grow by reading the Word of God. Sift everything you hear through the Word, or it will sift you. Are you listening? All those situations you are now facing will tear you apart or build you up. It depends on the way you look at them. This is how your character is developed. You were designed for such a time as this. If others are just cruel and unloving, as a believer, you know the Lord loves you unconditionally with no strings attached. And you have the power of the Holy Spirit inside of you as a helper for all your situations. Even if my mother and father abandon me, the Lord, Himself, will hold me close (Psalm 27:10). He can, and He will heal all of your emotions and wounds if you lay them at His feet and leave them there. Do not pick up what He has healed.

I declare: "I walk in the Spirit; I don't cater to the impulses of the flesh."

SEPTEMBER 23

If you insist on hanging onto lower thoughts, they will keep you down. We must stop the cycle of "stinking thinking." It poisons the brain faster than anything. Yes! And the fear we stir up paralyzes your healthy outlook on life. Negativity is a bad choice. It cannot stay. Have no fear of personal perfection. Why? Because you will never reach it, ever. Your words are keys; if you choose them correctly, you can close any negative mouth and unlock any heart, including your own. Wrong words are wrong words. And right words are right words even if no one is speaking to them. Arguing with a fool only now proves there are two. Also, there is a message of how others treat you with their body language. Pay attention. True love is built, not found. Easy will not change you. Change is the most powerful choice you can make to live and stay focused in the positive. You must make thinking positive thoughts a habit. It takes time to change. Do not grow weary, be patient and do the heavy lifting and the unpacking of that old rotten baggage. "Stinking thinking." He makes all things beautiful in His time (Ecclesiastes 3:11). Do not let anyone look down on you because you are young. But set an example for the believers in speech, in conduct, in love, in faith, and in purity (1 Timothy 4:12).

I declare: "A happy heart is good medicine, and a cheerful mind works healing."

SEPTEMBER 24

You are too hard on yourself! You are fearfully and wonderfully made. This is your winning season, and you are victorious. Stop stopping yourself. Go with what God is showing you to do. Stop doubting what He has prepared you to do. You believe the Word, and you read the Word. Those are your basic instructions for this life. Today is the youngest and oldest you will ever be. Celebrate you, your healthy life, your family, your workplace. You can get out of bed, drive your car, and earn a decent living. What is stopping you from feeling victorious? He can and will do wondrous things through you. Stop focusing on obstacles. He can put a light on a mountain and a stream in a desert. He is an awesome God. Everything you need is already in your heart. Forget the former things. If you keep thinking about them, it wears a pattern in your brain and stops you from thinking about your future. Do not dwell on the past. For He is doing a new thing. He is making a way in that desert. God directs your steps (Isaiah 43:18–19).

I declare: "I am determined and confident! I am not afraid or discouraged, for the Lord my God is with me wherever I go."

SEPTEMBER 25

Never forget that your mind plays the most important role for your victory. You must be bold in the Holy Spirit. You must think on purpose to think powerful thoughts. Passive thinking is dangerous. The devil hates the Word. That is why we must read it out loud. Ephesians 6:10–20 is a powerful way to start your day against the enemy of your soul. The devil will flee. Resist the devil and stand firm for your healing, your deliverance, and your situation. Ask the Lord to help stir you up and especially when you feel passive. You and I have authority over our lives through the *powerful* Word of God. If you do not feel like reading the Word out loud, that is a sure *sign* that you need to know. It is your sword against the tricks of the devil. The Word, the blood of Jesus, your *praise*, and your prayers are your tools against what is coming against you. This will lead you to victory. Declare: I am victorious. I am more than a conqueror. I am healed. I am delivered. I am set free. Think purposefully today. Guard your thoughts and words. My favorite tool is only *speak* what you want to happen. Your words are powerful. Speak life. Speak love. Speak healing. Or put the zipper on. Every word spoken will bear fruit for tomorrow, good or bad!

I declare: "I am victorious. I am more than a conqueror. I am healed. I am delivered. I am set free."

SEPTEMBER 26

Some things just drain the *"nice"* right out of you! Boost your happiness for free. Happiness is the new wealth. Be "flawsome." Embrace your flaws and believe you are still awesome. Reach out and connect with loved ones. Start a new goal and research new information about it. Watch an old movie. Go for a brisk walk. Exercise. Volunteer. Enrich your life. Bake or cook up something from an old family recipe. Declutter. Listen to your favorite music. Have a self-care day. Unplug from everything. It will be a challenge, but it will reboot your brain. Happiness is merely an inside job. Money does not buy happiness; it comes from the simple sweet things in life. Just sit down and read a good book. Push yourself until you succeed. Feeling down? Try the reboot. Do you know your worth? Transform your life with great self-care habits. This is a sure way to get out of a rut. Do not wait; you may have to get out of your own way. Things get better with change. Rise up, take courage, and do it (Ezra 10:4). Love keeps no records of wrongs (1 Corinthians 13:5). You will draw others if you refuse to be tainted by the world.

I declare the blessing of the Lord—it makes me (truly) rich, and He adds no sorrow with it.

SEPTEMBER 27

Taming the tongue is an ongoing battle. Be not wise in your own eyes (Proverbs 3:7). Do good to and speak well of the offender. Stop celebrating failures. Now. Today. Treat everyone the exact way you expect to be treated. Even if you do not agree with what they do or say, your attitude is going to help you. Stop trying to figure them out. Be that person with a beautiful mind. The right people hear you differently. Having the right attitude and mindset can literally change your entire life. What are you waiting for? New life, chapter one, will feel good. A sharp tongue can cut your own throat. Guard those words. Do not fear what others say. A complaining tongue reveals ungratefulness. Fools vent anger. Don't allow your tongue to outrun your brain. Wiser people speak less. The things you say about others say a lot about you. Who cares if you are beautiful if your tongue is ugly? No one can tame the tongue but God (James 3:8). Death and life are in the power of the tongue (Proverbs 18:21). Speak with wisdom. Watch your mouth; it will keep you from trouble. "Lord, I pray that You keep a guard over my mouth; may I be an encourager, a people builder, and a kind heart with powerful words to help others today."

If our tongues were made of glass, how carefully would we speak? Think before you speak. I am thinking.

I declare: "I trust in, rely on, and am confident in You, Lord; I say, 'You are my God.'"

SEPTEMBER 28

The only way the devil can get authority over you is if you start believing his lies. If you allow it. Every assignment from the enemy that is against you shall fall in the name of Jesus. If you must hurt others to feel powerful, then that makes you a weak human. Bullying is not cool. Rudeness is a weak person's imitation of their strength. Do not take this personally; stay silent. Set the example. You treat others with respect, even those who are rude. I choose daily to be kind. It makes my heart happy. I still believe I am fierce. But I choose to wear the zipper and trust the Lord. For the battles in life belong to Him. Do not look shaky; stay on the high road. Declare: I am passionate. I am creative. I do not have all the answers.

I will not be around others who make me feel less than I am. Be a person who loves and laughs. Stay kind and keep your ambition. Have confidence and class; fear only God. Stay about your own business and believe you are entering your winning season. Word of advice: Everyone will not see eye to eye, so they may not understand your mission. And that is okay. You know you are unstoppable. Know your worth and add the tax. Be in love with the person in the mirror. And you are still standing.

I declare: "I am passionate. I am creative. I do not have all the answers. I will not be around others who make me feel less than I am."

SEPTEMBER 29

Life will always be challenging. Do not worry. God is bigger. All of this is temporary. Pray before you keep overthinking. This will change how you age! Breathe. Do not lose your spark. Do not let the blues make you feel uncomfortable. You can lie to yourself about what is going on. Whatever you asked for in prayer this morning, God's got you. God is a restorer. You cannot fix it. But the Lord sure can. God is for you. Everything can change when you call on the name of Jesus. You can never exaggerate the greatness of God. Never. Welcome. I feel like this is breakthrough season. Believe right now what you have prayed for. Repeat your prayer to God right now. The devil loves when you are silent in prayer. There is not one moment when God is not in control. Sometimes when we feel there is no hope, God shows up to show us His power. Sometimes, we just want things to go right, simple things, a new heart, a new spirit (Ezekiel 36:25–27). Praise is the power to lighten our heaviest burden. The Holy Spirit is your helper, comforter, encourager, and counselor.

I declare: "In You, Lord, do I hope; You will answer, Lord my God."

SEPTEMBER 30

Ask yourself? What are you thinking today? Remember, you cannot hide your thoughts; sooner or later, they will surface. There is one thing for sure; you cannot hide your true feelings. Your body language will tell on you. Your eyes, eyebrows, hands, and feet tell what you are saying. That is why we must protect our minds; no thought is ever careless. Your body will pick up what you are thinking. Your body always tells the truth. Keep yourself in the agape love of God as you wait for our Lord. Let Him fill you with mercy, which leads to the life of the age to come. In perfect peace (Jude 1:21). Working out of love means every area of you must show love. Your attitude precedes you before you even enter a room. Be careful what you are thinking; your body is smarter than you think. I raise a hallelujah. Think of yourself smart. It is important to think according to the love of God. And God loves the unlovely; He loves everything about everyone. We must be salt and light. No judgment allowed. It is mindless to judge unless you judge yourself. Separate yourself from your problems. Prayer is powerful. Ask, believe, and receive (Matthew 7:7). Walk by faith and not by what you see. It will take practice.

I declare: "I have supernatural, preternatural, and paranormal favor all over me from God."

October

From the fruit of their lips people enjoy good things, but the unfaithful have an appetite for violence. Those who guard their lips preserve their lives, but those who speak rashly will come to ruin.

Proverbs 13:2–3

Your words are powerful. Be careful what you speak.

OCTOBER 1

Some hearts are dedicated but not devoted. Devotion pre-serves your relationship with God. He will speak to you. Devotion protects your marriage. It is called *self-control.* Life taught me. Experiences closed my mouth. Last year changed me. This year will be the "breakthrough" year. God has never run out of miracles; you are next. God is not ignoring you. He has a reason for every season. There is a huge purpose behind what you are facing. Stop talking. Allow God to work. Manipulation will not work. We must respect and respond with hope. He is in control. Your heart cannot stay troubled (John 14:1). Complaining is a waste of time. Your words have power, so use them wisely. Do not let your emotions overrule you. Stop chasing what is not working. Your successes will begin with your self-discipline. Everything starts with you. The life in front of you now is far more important than the life you have already lived behind you. Read that slowly. Do not compare. You cannot care of what you did not do. It is fine. Maybe you have been stuck because you are pushing a door that says, "Pull open." Your faith moves mountains, and your doubt keeps creating them. Until God opens another door for you, praise Him in the hallway. What was meant for evil, God meant for good (Genesis 50:20).

I declare: "I will keep silent and discerning if I hold my tongue."

OCTOBER 2

Stop immediately! You already know you cannot fix your problems or anyone else's. Just relax and trust that God is working on it. Relax, God has got this. Think of all that they are instead of all that they are not. The best weight you will ever lose is that weight of another person's opinion. Remember, salt and sugar look the same. Develop an attitude of gratitude. Hush until you heal. Attending unnecessary arguments is not a good idea either. Cling to what is good (Romans 12:9). If you are looking for that one very special person that can change your entire life, look in the mirror. If you decide to quit anything, quit waiting, and quit excuses too. A wise person knows you can learn something new from anyone. New habits. New life. All loyalty is returned; stay loyal. The best thing about hard times is you get to see what you are made of and others too. Do not let the world change your God-given morals. Do not lower your standards. Think of others (Philippians 2:4). Choose to develop a mindset of possibilities over yourself. Whenever you feel unloved, unimportant, or insecure, remember to whom you belong (Ephesians 2:19–22).

I declare: "I choose to look at the interest of others instead of my own interests."

OCTOBER 3

Your deliverance will come from discerning what is inside of you, not what is inside of me. Fear is a liar. Only I can change me. And only you can change you. The very last thing the enemy wants you to do is to get in the presence of God. "Put on" the garment of praise for the spirit of heaviness. God is going to use the very thing that was meant to destroy you to deliver you (1 Samuel 17:1). Jehovah Jireh is your provider. Jehovah Nissi is your banner. Jehovah Shalom is your peace. He is the Lord of all. Intercession prayer is the highest form of love. It will overpower the evil influences that have bound that person. It is deliverance from Satan. Pray against the spirit of Jezebel; it is a manipulation spirit, not from God. Pray and do not give up (Luke 18:1). Do not let sadness tighten your shackles. Try again, this time with God. Fasting breaks the chains and deliverance. Break ungodly soul ties. Declare: I curse out every evil spirit in my life that attempts to stop my blessings. I rebuke every thought or negative word spoken against me and break every chain. In Jesus' name. Feed your mind with the Word of God. Prayer. Stewardship. Good works. Holiness (1 Peter 4:11).

I declare: "I curse out every evil spirit in my life that attempts to stop my blessings. I rebuke every thought or negative word spoken against me and break every chain."

OCTOBER 4

Being wise is knowing what to overlook. It is a mindset.

Staying teachable is a blessing. Learning from mistakes means you are really living your life. Be a risk taker; just living life can be risky. If you are still in the same problem, check and see if it is not your own attitude. Focus your energy on helping others out; get your focus off yourself. Work from your heart today. Your attitude is your greatest asset. Think about this; problems give meaning to life. Your greatest weakness is your unbelief. Choose to see the glass half full. Spend time today to sit back and dwell on your blessings and the people in your life that bring you joy, hope, and love. Choose to see possibilities. Change your thoughts. You matter. Your thoughts and actions matter too. We all think differently, and that is okay. Our differences complement one another. You are different, and so am I. Let us stir up one another's minds to energetic effort in love and good works. We must encourage one another even more as we see the great day coming closer (Hebrews 10:24–25).

I declare: "And let us consider how we may encourage one another on toward love and good deeds."

OCTOBER 5

Nothing you have is because of luck or chance. It is all because of the favor of God's grace. Even though you may get fed up, you have got to keep your head up. He opens the doors for you that no one can ever close (Revelation 3:8). God can turn those private prayers into public blessings. I do not want to miss one word He speaks. Keep praying for your family. God is hearing you. No complaining or murmuring. It stops the hand of God. What is your prayer today? Pray until your situation changes. Every day, God thinks of you. Your prayer request is about to become a praise report. Just one small act of kindness could mean the world to someone. Pray for healing overall and never wish anyone pain. You cannot live with broken pieces; it will destroy who you are. Never be cruel. Do not fool yourself; you will pick what you plant. Strong people live in forgiveness. Do not be ashamed of your weakness. I grew strong in the Lord through all my weaknesses, insecurities, and rejection. God has shown me over and over never to be a prisoner of the past. Emotions are from your history. Praise is your future. Stay in praise! Switch your mentality from being emotional to staying in praise and thanksgiving. Your answers in life are in your praise.

I declare: "I will praise the Lord all my life; I will sing praise to my God as long as I live."

OCTOBER 6

A true worshiper will always turn pain into prayer. Broken people turn into spiritual warriors. Once you get control over your mind, anything is possible. Pain sharpens, and iron sharpens iron. You find your worth inside your spirit man from the power of the Holy Spirit. Learn to love the sound of your feet, walking away from the opinions, drama, and things others say to you or about you. In order to love who you are, you cannot hate the experiences that showed you how not to be and what not to do. Remain humble, stay grateful. This has shaped you to hustle, not to hate or be jealous. I have learned it is not your job to like me; it is my job to like me and grow and walk in agape love, making a beautiful difference in the lives of others. And it is your job to like you. Be the type of person who knows that your crown is not on your head but in your soul. Disconnect and enjoy yourself. I am built from every mistake, every setback, and every hard lesson that I have lived through. Staying thankful. I have a purpose-driven warrior attitude to do something great for the world. I am on a mission. No one is you. And that is your power. Rejoice. Love like Jesus. Be strong and do not give up, for your work will be rewarded (2 Chronicles 15:7).

I declare: "I will be completely humble, gentle, and patient."

OCTOBER 7

The enemy thought he was going to destroy you when you were young. The enemy is looking for an opening, a tiny crack to come in. He comes to kill, steal, and destroy. Right now! Trust God with whatever is weighing you down. Do not let the opinions of others weigh you down. Turn your obsessive thoughts into powerful prayer. There is a huge value in you, or else the enemy would not be attacking you. Take up the sword of the spirit and fight the enemy. You are not abandoned, forgotten, or unloved. You *are* redeemed and purchased by the love of God. Any negativity that has come to you must be returned to the sender in Jesus' name! No weapon. Never give the enemy legal rights to your gifting. If anyone looks down on someone, they are not from God. Be wise in the Word, not your own eyes. You can get fooled if others are not saturated in the Holy Spirit. Salt and sugar look the same. If your inner peace is gone, the enemy stole it. The joy of the Lord is your strength (Jeremiah 8:10). When the time is right, the Lord will make it happen (Isaiah 60:22). God intended for good, so shake it off. When our thoughts and words are positive, our hearts will be too. If you are fighting with others, you cannot fight the enemy. It is a trick of the enemy. Be still and trust God.

I declare: "Thanks be to God, who gives me the victory (making me a conqueror) through my Lord Jesus Christ."

OCTOBER 8

The more frustrated you feel, the more fruitful you will think. This is not a breakdown; I call it a breakthrough. There is one thing always certain about life; it is called change. The pain will leave when you learn to let it all go. Stop holding on to your history; it is too emotional and will cost you the expense of your destiny. Anchor your spirit man in the Word. Celebrate and enjoy the relationship with yourself. By enduring pain and releasing it, you will grow in greatness and become a new creature in Christ. God is going to show you His power in that problem. There is a purpose in this, bigger than you. Your most powerful tool is your mind. Pray for God's wisdom. Faith must pass this test to move on. Growth means choosing to stay happy over history and not looking back. Delight yourself, your mind, your will, and your emotions in the Lord. Completely. And He will give you the desires of your heart (Psalm 37:4). Loving is for a lifetime. It is also a part of your daily journey, starting with you. How can you show your love for the Lord today? Autumn shows us how beautiful it is to let things go.

I declare: "I think about sticking with things because the thoughts of the diligent tend only to plenty."

OCTOBER 9

Accept not knowing all the answers because God controls everything. Take responsibility for your choices and the outcomes. Don't expect others to agree. Be responsible for your part and allow others to be responsible for theirs. The everyone-is-a-winner mentality is not one of accountability. Be responsible. You are the product of your decision, not anyone else. Be the better everything. Leadership is responsibility in all areas. It is not your fault if you were born in a negative situation; if you die in that same negative situation, it is on you. Do not blame anyone for your dysfunction. Life is about moving on. Everyone talks about being responsible, yet most fail. Start by taking responsibility for your thoughts and words. I am not a product of my situations. I am a product of my own goals and decision to follow the Lord. Responsibility is your power. You and you alone are responsible for the energy you bring wherever you go. You are the cause and the solution to the matters in your own life. Accountability, responsibility, and loyalty are the core values of spiritual maturity. Pay careful attention to your own work, for then you will get the satisfaction of job well done, and you will not compare yourself to anyone else, for we are responsible for our own conduct (Galatians 6:4–5).

I declare: "I am living the life of the Spirit because the Holy Spirit dwells within me."

OCTOBER 10

We may seek different ways of solving our problems. But until we change what is inside of us, we will never change the outcome. "Teach me Your ways, Lord, so I may honor You. Amen."

Habits, good habits, become natural. Did you know that decluttering is a beautiful way to spark up your joy, making you feel like it is a fresh start kind of day? Clean and clear up your own space no matter where it is: Work, home, car, closet, your desk, or even the fridge. Trust yourself. There are things you can live without. Impossible? Wait a minute; it is just an opinion. Excellence is an attitude. You were not born to be mediocre. Leadership is not about a position. It is about your own personal passion for excellence, making that huge difference wherever you go. And it is not impossible. Excellence is a habit. If serving others is below you, then leadership is not you. You lead by example. Get out of the box you have been raised in, or you will never understand the bigger picture of the bigger world. Calmness is a supernatural power. Readers, be advised and remember the devil is a liar. You are not afraid of the future; you are afraid of repeating the past. Your attention, please: This life of yours is 100 percent your responsibility. If God is for us, who can be against us (Romans 8:31)?

I declare: "Whatever you do, work heartily, as for the Lord and not for men."

OCTOBER 11

Parenting, a tough responsibility, is a bittersweet job. We want and do what we think is best for our children as they become their own people with conflicting tastes and desires. I took the nos and the differences personally. At times nothing works or gets better. In fact, things can get worse. Sound familiar? Good news! You can't parent without God's supernatural support. My hardest days of parenting were praying earnestly on my knees. God loves our children more than we do. He created them all on purpose to be unique. He designed us to stay strong in unconditional love for our children. Be patient like the Lord is with you. It is a struggle. I survived through prayer, and so will you. Celebrate your children. Tough situations create warrior adults. We all need direction and will get it from the Rock. Ask, believe, and receive. You have not because you ask not. Tough days feel never-ending and overwhelming. Get up, brush yourself off, and seek the Lord (Matthew 7:7). Love and forgive yourself. If you pray about it, God works on it. Release peace over your home. Dry your eyes and be encouraged. Trust the Lord. Faith in God is stronger than frustration. Be refreshed.

I declare: "I am blessed. I am patient. I am walking this out in love. I am chosen. I am training my child in the way he shall go, and he will not depart from it (Proverbs 22:6)."

OCTOBER 12

If your mind is unhealthy, it doesn't matter how strong you are, how many sermons you listen to, or how many green drinks you consume. If you desire to live a healthy life, retrain your brain to think healthy thoughts, say kind things, and treat others well. Your body is the temple of the Holy Spirit, the spirit God gave you, so you won't belong to your selfish ways. You are an expensive purchase; glorify God in your body and in all you do (1 Corinthians 6:19–20). Pray about the pleasures of the flesh. Take responsibility for the power of your thoughts and words. God wants to use you to touch this hurting world, not to injure or hurt others. He calls us to help restore, encourage, and be salt and light. This broken world needs you. Stop rehearsing your hurts and blaming your broken past. You have been delivered. Spiritual maturity is the spirit man over the mind man. Refresh your mind. Nail the broken pieces to the bottom of the cross, once and for all, and leave them there. Be mindful of what separates you from the true love of God. I never want to leave His presence. I wake up thinking what the Lord will have me do today. I fear not seeking Him first. Are you making yourself approachable?

I declare: "I am a true seeker of Jesus; more than anything, I want to be like Him. Nothing else will do. I nail my flesh to the cross and crucify myself. I long to be a vessel full of the Holy Spirit."

OCTOBER 13

You can point and blame or pray and intercede. When others ask, "What do you do?" Your answer is, "Whatever it takes." You must control what you are thinking. Of course, I talk to myself; I need the pep talk too. And so do you. Those who are different are those who make the difference. Well done is better than well said. Your life is what your thoughts make it. An attitude that is of positive expectations is the true mark of a super personality. I am that which I believe I am. Surround yourself with others that will force you to grow. And remember, do not waste a good mistake. Grow from it. You are a part of everything you have met. Love others so radically that they know you are filled with the love of God. Do not worry; the people who know the least about you always have the most to say. Let that go today. Declare: No matter what comes my way, I can do it. It is challenging to stay in the will of God. Be doers of the Word, and not hearers only, deceiving yourself (James 1:22). Open your heart and invite Jesus into every situation because when God enters the scene, miracles will happen. Align yourself today to hang with others who fit into your destiny, not your history. No matter how you feel, dress up, show up, and never give up. Never. Do not fizzle. Listen to God-given advice and accept instruction, and in the end, you will be wise (Proverbs 19:20).

I declare: "No matter what comes my way, I can do it."

OCTOBER 14

We do not choose to live one foot in marriage and one foot out. Marriages stay blessed when we stay devoted and committed. He who calls you faithful will also do it (1 Thessalonians 5:24). God will help you if you believe He has called you to your situation, as a spouse, as a parent, at your place of work, or in your current circumstance. God works through everything that touches your life for your good, but you must believe He will and not take it in your own hands. You must trust Him right now to supply your needs. It is not the plan of God for you to lay awake all night, tossing and turning, worrying how things will work out. He is the Creator of heaven and earth and you as well. Whether you need emotional healing, a new job, a new friend, or your marriage restored, set the issue before the Lord and let Him provide what you need. It will be challenging to remain patient because your faith will be tested. Commit to listening to what the Lord is saying to you. In His presence, only let His Word speak to you so you won't get confused. Confusion is handpicked from the enemy to get you on the wrong path of destruction over your home, which can last a lifetime. Stay strong in the Lord, and the power of His might stand against the enemy; your family will thank you for it (Ephesians 6:10–20).

I declare: "I trust You, God, to restore my relationships."

OCTOBER 15

Steps away from your true path are pits of self-pity. Keep your eyes on God. I know I have said this before, "You cannot change anyone"; you can change only you. The wonderful news is when you do change yourself, everything changes. You become happy all over. Your relationships are so much happier. Happy people have common values. They are not moved by negativity, rudeness, criticism, or opposition from others. They are completely happy with themselves. Habits of happy people: Ignore foolishness, listen more, learn about new goals, *laugh*, get up super early, no entitlement thinking, and stay grateful. Of course, they put God first when they start their day. Declare: I am annoyingly positive and optimistic. I am as happy as I make up my mind to be. The first step to happiness is not to keep telling your sad story. Eventually, you will not be living a sad life. Seasons change. People do not. Problems are a part of life. Speak healing, victory, strength, and blessings over your whole life in Jesus' mighty name. The depth of your praise will determine the magnitude of your breakthrough. Only be moved by the Word and the hand of God, not by what you see, hear, or feel. The Word will work if you work the Word.

I declare: "I am annoyingly positive and optimistic."

OCTOBER 16

The devil will do his best to distract you because he knows he can't have your heart. Distractions and excuses lurk after you. Opportunities will not. Distractions waste your energy. You must stop being distracted by people, places, and things that conflict with your goals. Disconnect. If you are not committed to your goals, you will be distracted by everything. Just because you do it well does not mean it's not a heavy load to carry. What you do makes a difference, and you must decide what kind of difference you want to make. We are all human until we find the distractions of race, politics, and social status. Do not let the love of God in your life be a distraction. You have the power within you to rise above whatever is bringing you down. Get rid of distractions. Your assignment by God is too important, and your time is too valuable to be distracted by the negativity of others. I declare: "I keep my mind focused on peace, harmony, health, and agape love. Then, I cannot be distracted by others, choices, opinions, doubts, and fears." It has got to go in Jesus' name. That unhealthy stuff kills more dreams than failure ever will. Satan's powerful tool to use against good people is distraction. Ignore the noise; stay focused. When the enemy cannot destroy you, his job is to distract you. Distractions be gone in Jesus' name. Now.

I declare: "I keep my mind focused on peace, harmony, health, and agape love."

OCTOBER 17

Prayer is not the preparation for the battle; it is the battle. You only lose if you give up. Declare: I am not going to give up. Information overload is a distraction; it will dilute your focus and get you off your game plan. I have learned now that while those who speak about one's misery usually hurt, and those who keep silent hurt more. Saying you are okay is so much easier than explaining the reasons why you are not. It will take one minute to push yourself out of bed and read the Word of God. But it takes a whole life to regret and move on for not seeking Him first. He is the ultimate life-changer through prayer. It takes a real man to live for God—a lot more man than to live for evil. While others are sleeping, study. While others are loafing, work. Prepare, dream, and pray while others sit back and wish. You must do the hard work. Live better. Just like alkaline water kills cancer, the Word of God kills evil. Refuse to be average. The truth is that if you gave 100 percent, you would get 100 percent back. The truth is everything in life is all up to you, 100 percent. My prayer for you today is that revival fire hits your home and family. In Jesus' mighty name, amen. Stand for your family. God is the restorer. He is in control. Stop thinking you are.

I declare: "I am not going to give up."

OCTOBER 18

Your anxiety is you are worried about your future. Nothing is hidden from God. He knows all about you. Jesus is the life; the Holy Spirit is the breath. He will breathe right through you with the power of Christ. You cannot show the power of Christ being indifferent and cold. The Holy Spirit is fire: it shines, it glows, and it is warm. It is to crown the King with our actions. Again, we must have mental discipline.

> *Now to him who is able to do more than we ask or imagine, according to his power that is at work within us, the Holy Spirit, to him be the glory in the church and in Christ throughout all generations, forever and ever.*
>
> *Ephesians 3:20–21 (NIV)*

To be filled with God means that you are set free. Joy, peace, and blessings are strengthened with the character of God, renewed in your mind, and transformed by His mighty power. He whom the Son sets free is free indeed. What do you need? Is there anything too hard for God?

I declare: "In the day of my trouble, I will call upon You, for You will answer me" (Psalm 86:7, NKJV).

OCTOBER 19

Those who live close to God develop an inner aliveness that makes them seem youthful in spite of their years. They can smile at others with His joy and love them with His love. That's how you recognize the love of God. You have no time to battle egos. You should respectfully not care. Have you ever met the human version of a headache? Honesty is what saves everyone's time. A person who values you would never put themselves in a position to lose you. Your relationship with God is your number one focus. If you take care of that, you can trust Him to take care of everything and everyone else. Pray that others' words will not blind you from their behavior. How others treat people tells all, not their words but their actions. Until you get yourself healed through the Word of God and the supernatural power of the Holy Spirit, you will be toxic to anyone who tries to help or love you. We need to get serious with the Word. Tomorrow will not be any different unless you start today. The real test is being kind to unkind people. Your path is more difficult because your calling is higher. The Lord has heard your prayers and seen your tears. He will heal you (2 Kings 20:5).

I declare: "According to God's Word, I have been made the righteousness of God in Christ."

OCTOBER 20

Nothing will bring you greater peace than minding your own business right now. God is teaching you how to stay silent in this frustrating season. The truth is, the less you say, the more He will move. Stay silent! If being hurt caused you to leave your church and lose faith in God, then your faith was in people, not God. Read that again. You cannot stop others' opinions of you. And you do not need them to know the truth; you only need to remind yourself about the truth. It is never about you. It just may be about what they think about themselves. The act of getting strong does not start in the gym. It will always start in your head with your own thinking. For God is not a God of confusion but of peace (1 Corinthians 14:33). The devil whispered in my ear, "You are not strong enough to withstand this storm." I whispered in the devil's ear, "I am a child of God, a person of faith, a warrior of Christ; with Him, I am the storm." When God's warriors get down on their knees, the battle is not over, it has just begun in victory.

I declare: "I am a child of God, a person of faith, a warrior of Christ!"

OCTOBER 21

Problems are a part of life, but unforgiveness chains you to your past. The poison of it will rob your present situation.

That chain of unforgiveness is not worth the price you pay. Unforgiveness is really hatred. It makes you a bitter person. You cannot be bitter and expect yourself to live a sweet life. Keep uprooting that spirit of unforgiveness; it is a bitter root. Forgive as the Lord forgave you (Colossians 3:13). I have forgiven others who were not even sorry. But I am completely set free. Do not be afraid to allow the Holy Spirit to reveal any unforgiveness or bitterness you may have buried. The longer it is hidden, the stronger it becomes, and the harder your heart will be. It creates negative emotions and energy. Unforgiveness opens doors to evil and sickness. The best antidote against bitterness is pure forgiveness. It will kill you, not them. Release and let it go. I have never met a thankful person who was bitter. The heaviest thing you will carry is a grudge. Practice God's presence. The moment you forgive, you are set free. Forgive them even if they are not sorry. Your chains are gone. Forgiveness changes your future, not your past. Pray for the people who have hurt you. Forgiveness withheld is recovery delayed. Less bitter, more glitter. Unforgiveness is toxic; it will ruin your life and age you. All things are working for my good (Romans 8:28).

I declare: "If I forgive people of their sins, my heavenly Father will also forgive me."

OCTOBER 22

Do what you can in the here and now. Make life beautiful. Your story goes on even if someone will not be in the next season of your life. We grieve with hope (1 Thessalonians 4:13). They did not leave your life; God just moved them. Small things can trigger grief: a look, a picture, a fragrance, or a song. Within a few seconds, like a time machine, you are brought back to that exact moment. And yet grief is different for everyone, even though common to all. Loss changes you and your life forever. Grief will not follow a calendar, time, or alarm clock. It has no expiration date. Your mind knows it; now, you need to feel it in your heart. It takes a while. Cry in the shower, sob in the pillow, and keep praying. You will make it. You only understand loss after it has placed its hands on someone we love because we grieve the life we planned and envisioned with them. If you feel weary or broken because of a loss, simply give God everything you are struggling with each morning. Now you have already won. Keep going; you will make it through. Be the things you love the most about the people who are gone. Time does not heal; God does. You will be fine; you have God. God wants you to enjoy your life now, not when. Be that person who makes it easy for others to believe in God.

I declare: "When I cry out, the Lord hears and delivers me out of all my troubles."

OCTOBER 23

Be brave, be strong, and be courageous. Do not be afraid, do not be disappointed. For the Lord your God will be with you wherever you go (Joshua 1:9). If you are reading this today, may the Lord remove your pain, problems, alcoholism, addictions, pornography, fear, doubt, and worry. And replace them with healing, answers, happiness, joy, and deep satisfaction that only God can give. Peace passes all understanding over your life right now to get up and do what you need to do to be set free in Him. If you must delete certain numbers, do so now. If you must delete people from your social media or contact list, do it now. Life is too short to be wasting valuable time. God has an amazing plan over your life. Be bold; take that risk. Have no regrets to live life on purpose, to be a better you. You are so worth it. If you do not get in your Bible, the enemy will get in your business. God has more in store for you than you can ever imagine (Ephesians 3:20). Be my strength every morning (Isaiah 33:2b). The struggle is real, but so is God. The Lord is greater than the giants you face (1 John 4:4). Faith is refusal to panic. "The name of the Lord is a strong tower; the righteous run to it and are safe" (Proverbs 18:10, NKJV).

I declare: "I pray to God that I will not be overcome by temptation."

OCTOBER 24

Wisdom is when you have a lot to say, but you choose to remain silent. Do not be annoyed when someone does something to you and expects you to be okay with it when they would not be okay with it if it was done to them. If you constantly treat a person a lot better than they treat you, it might be time to change seasons. To survive, do what seasons do, change. Just like seasons, people change too. It is important for you to live each season of your life. Before you start this day, pray over yourself with belief: "There is an anointing on my life, and I believe, Lord, You will go before me this day, making the crooked places straight. Angels are being released on my behalf to direct and guide me. *Abba* Father, I believe every weapon formed against me shall not prosper."

Only fake flowers are flawless. Be such a beautiful blessing that people crave to be around you, not repel you. You are not called to be like other Christians: you are called to be like Christ. If you are still waiting on God, do what waiters do: *serve.* Your joy cannot be found in a person, place, or thing. Do not be a part-time Christian who demands a full-time God. The principal part of your faith is patience. The very breath of God is in you (Job 33:4).

I declare: "The blessing of the Lord makes me (truly) rich, and He adds no sorrow with it."

OCTOBER 25

Daily you are being presented with choices. Declare: Today, by the supernatural power of the Holy Spirit, I can change my story. Make it happen. Shock everyone. You have outgrown the old you. You will remain uncomfortable because your old life does not fit anymore. Stop living an unhealthy lifestyle. Fear tricks us into thinking we are living a boring life when we follow the Lord. Sometimes, you just must be done; not mad, not upset, just done with the silliness. Sometimes, you never know the damage you have done until that same thing is done to you. The most painful thing is to lose yourself in that painful process. One thing is certain: you will have to answer to God for the way you live your life and treat others. How you are treated is how they feel about you. Oh, and your soul mate is not another person's spouse. Believing you are a good person and being one are two completely different things. If you know you can live better, then live better. Whenever you feel unloved, unimportant, insecure, or rejected, remember to whom you belong to, Jesus (Ephesians 2:19–22).

I declare: "Today, by the supernatural power of the Holy Spirit, I will change my story."

OCTOBER 26

Crying is speaking when your words cannot explain your pain. Silly, expecting too much from others again? Appreciate the good people, for they are hard to find in life. I have got a thing for genuine people. You must learn who is gold and who is gold-plated. Just keep it all real. Weaknesses, like failure, only prove you are real. Failure is one of the most important parts of growth and developing resilience. You have not failed. But you did discover 1,000 ways something will not work. It is about your attitude. If you do not like something, change it. Stop complaining. If you cannot change it, change your attitude. A beautiful attitude is solid gold. My height is five feet two inches, but my attitude is seven feet seven inches. Watch your attitude; it is the very first thing people notice about you. Be valuable. Your attitude reflects your heart. Shoes and people will hurt you if they are not your size. If you wake up feeling fragile, remember that it is not God. Trust Him to be everything you need today. God is my strength (Habakkuk 3:19).

I declare: "The Sovereign Lord is my strength; He makes my feet like the feet of a deer; He enables me to tread on the heights."

OCTOBER 27

Your own story is filled with shattered dreams, broken promises, and ugly truths. Because of God, it has changed into major breakthroughs, peaceful thinking, and grace that has changed your soul man. Only two things will ever change in your life: your outlook and your age. The only thing that can make you unhappy is your own thoughts. Do not make moves without praying about it first. One thing I know, those prayers work! I mind my own business and talk to God a lot. Let God write your love story. Some disconnections can bless your life. Stop ignoring the signs you asked God to show you. I am a huge fan of God's work. If you do not let the past die, then it will not let you live. Start living. Working together means success. You will not win in life if you are losing in your thinking. Rejoice with hope, stay patient in this tribulation season, and be consistent in your prayer life (Romans 12:12). "For God has not given us a spirit of fear, but of power and of love and of a sound mind" (2 Timothy 1:7, NKJV).

I declare: "For the Spirit God gave us does not make us timid but gives us power, love, and self-discipline."

OCTOBER 28

Are you addicted to painful patterns? As you grow in God's grace, your patterns will be broken. Negative talk releases negative chemicals in your brain and takes over your body, causing sickness and disease. Negative thinking does the same. Guard your words and thoughts. Guilt, unconfessed sin, can be painful spiritually and bring on fear, shame, and stress. Give thanks to the Lord. Free yourself from hidden pain. Being sorry or crying out is not repentance. A cheerful heart is good medicine for your body and soul. Let good cheer fill your heart and radiate from your face. Fill your mind with gratitude and Praise the Lord for all He has already done. It is not about what you eat and drink that damages you. It is your speaking and thinking that can ruin your life. True repentance is turning from your wicked ways. Have unconditional surrender to God. Declare: I am a mighty child of God. I am loved. I am valuable. I Am strong in the Lord. I am bold and courageous. I am an empowering influence. I am directed by the power of the Holy Spirit. I heard the voice of the Lord saying, "'Whom shall I send, and who will go for Us?' [Compassion for the lost.] Then I said, 'Here am I! Send me'" (Isaiah 6:8, NKJV).

I declare: "I am a mighty child of God. I am loved. I am valuable. I am strong in the Lord. I am bold and courageous. I am an empowering influence. I am directed by the power of the Holy Spirit."

OCTOBER 29

Everything in life begins in the mind! Be thankful for the ones who broke down your walls without you even noticing. They then helped you rebuild your walls by adding windows to let pure, beautiful, warm, and everlasting sunshine in. Your prayer is the world's greatest wireless connection ever. You will become ten times more attractive, not by your looks but by your acts of kindness, respect, honesty, and loyalty when no one is looking. Integrity is *everything*. Cheating is the most disrespectful, hurtful thing you can display in any area of your life. Protect your spirit from negativity. Feed your goals and new focus. Be thankful we do not look like what we have been through. Nourish to flourish. What we learn about love is taught by people who never really loved us. Can I get an amen? Focus on people who inspire you. Emotional health is not a weakness; it is wisdom. One simple rule: never lie. Always be honest (Proverbs 12:22). Keep your promises (Romans 4:21). Be kind and tenderhearted (Ephesians 4:32). Honor God in everything (Revelations 4:11). Protect your thoughts one word at a time!

I declare: "The Lord detests lying lips, but He delights in people who are trustworthy."

OCTOBER 30

You *can* do everything you think you cannot. Faith is forwarding all issues to Heaven right now. It is the Holy Spirit who gives life. The flesh profits nothing. The words that I speak to you are spirit and life (John 6:63). Your humility and your fear of the Lord will be riches, honor, and life (Proverbs 22:4). Declare: I am an overcomer. What is the best part about this life? You have a new opportunity every morning to fill your reserve with empowering words, thoughts, and actions. Slay your own strongholds daily. Do not start today with that old, dirty-thinking mindset. Do not let others pollute your vision. You are not given a bad life or a good life. You were given life. Shout out to those who have not felt okay lately but get up every day with an empowering mindset and refuse to quit. You do not lose good people; you lose people who are not good for you. The power of "yet." Repeat: The best is "yet" to come.

I declare: "I am an overcomer."

OCTOBER 31

As I unclutter, I free myself to the calling of my soul man. Mental clutter stops my soul. Every single day clear out something that does not serve you or your goals. If it's a thought or holes in your socks, it has got to go. Old ideas or toxic relationships must flee in Jesus' name. Bad habits cannot stay either. Detox your home. Eliminate instead of organizing. Clutter is anything that gets between you and life. Everything is 100 percent off when you do not buy it. All you need is less. Are you really living life, or are you just paying bills? The most complicated skill is to live simply. Do not try to fill an emotional gap by spending. Nothing will ever satisfy your soul like the Lord. It is not your salary that makes you rich; it is your spending habits. Remember, your living space is not a store. You do not need to save "just in case." He who buys what he does not need steals from himself, simplicity, more time, more joy, and more space. If you must buy one item, get rid of two. You may get eighty-five years of life; do not spend sixty-five years paying off a lifestyle. Stuff is not serving you if it is packed away on a shelf. If it costs you your peace, it is too expensive. Storage is not a solution. "Just in case" often becomes wasted space. Unblock yourself. Your whispers in the night give me wisdom showing me what to do next (Psalm 16:7).

I declare: "But all things should be done decently and in order."

November

Those who guard their mouths and their tongues keep themselves from calamity.

Proverbs 21:23 (NIV)

Your words are powerful. Be careful what you speak.

NOVEMBER 1

Remember, it is more about people who treat you badly than it is about you. Learn the secret of being satisfied in every situation. Start by acknowledging your worries and frustrations to God. Do not stop there; replace the negative news with possible possibilities. Simply pour out your heart to Him. You get cleansed by doing so. Continue seeking Him for answers, and be aware of asking others who are not seeking God. "Trust in the LORD with all your heart, and lean not on your own understanding" (Proverbs 3:5, NKJV). You are holy and blameless in His sight. God chose you before the foundation of the world to be holy and blameless (Ephesians 1:7). Set up your priorities daily. Your time and energy are limited. You have a huge, higher purpose here in the world. Do not get stuck by small thinking and others' finger-pointing. It must not pull you down. You are a child of the King. You belong to Him. He has called you out of darkness into His marvelous light. You are a chosen generation, a royal priesthood, and a holy nation. His own special person. He called you (1 Peter 2:9)! What keeps you chained up? Your thoughts of fear for the future? Remember this: He is helping you right now. He will never leave or forsake you. Seek Him (Matthew 6:34).

I declare: "I will find the Lord when I seek Him with all my heart and with all my soul."

NOVEMBER 2

What you do behind closed doors is who you are. Do not be offended by the truth. The truth will set you free. A broken person is not the same as an evil person. If you have a hidden agenda, you are not a broken person. Do not get annoyed or irritated; it is fuel to people who are evil. Everything you say can be used against you. It is more powerful and important to stay silent. Toxic people can and will manipulate a survivor. Stay calm. God designed you to manifest the destiny He spoke over you before the foundations of this earth. What are you waiting for? You will not have to present yourself in the light. Let God make all the moves and open all the doors. Put your total confidence in Him. Control must flee. The spirit of God resides within you. "Oh, Lord, let me hear You. Your sweet mercy cannot be held back from those who put their control in Your capable hands. I am a new creature. Redirect my thoughts, improve my vision, and give me clarity on what I need to focus on." A calm, undisturbed mind and heart are the life and health of the body, but envy, jealousy, and wrath are like rottenness of the bones (Proverbs 14:30).

I declare: "Because I listen diligently to the voice of the Lord my God, being watchful to do all His commandments that He commands me this day, the Lord my God will set me high above all the nations of the earth."

NOVEMBER 3

Do not let one thought, one word, or one action interfere with the Word of God. If He told you something, you must wait on Him to provide. Brokenness is a way to totally rely on Him. You are in a good place. My brokenness was my greatest blessing. He made me who I am today. Stay strong in Him. You will never have trouble with people who are filled with the power of the Holy Spirit. He wants us to stay so filled with His power so that we will not be short of gifts that He has freely given to us. It is truly a blessing to have a good time and enjoy your life with the gifts He has given to you. Stay in tune with the Holy Spirit for the encouragement and enjoyment in the Lord and not at the expense of anyone else. We must pray and use all our gifts wisely. We must ask ourselves, "What is our motive?" We must set forth to do the work of the Holy Spirit and be careful of deceptive voices. Pray! Many people are tricked by troubled voices. God is love. That means for all. You only need the Holy Spirit as your teacher. Do not be misled by a voice. Not only for your sake but for the sake of others. Do not believe every spirit, but test the spirits, see if they are of God (1 John 4:1).

I declare: "Faith comes by hearing, and hearing by the word of God" *(Romans 10:17, NKJV).*

NOVEMBER 4

Some of the best advice I have been given is, "Don't take criticism from people you would never go to for advice." If anything, some people just teach you how not to be. If there are people in your life you cannot speak the truth to, and you feel like you must walk on eggshells to avoid getting them upset, you are being controlled or manipulated. When others lose control over you, they will try to control how others see you. Pray for them and forgive quickly. You must always be who God created you to be without watering down your progress, success, or the way you have chosen to live. Put God first, regardless of those trials you are facing. Remember you are blessed, so you can be a blessing. This is going to be a big week for you. Declare: I am healed; I will see unexpected blessings and spiritual insight. I can do this. In Jesus' name. Only those who are unhappy with themselves are mean to others. A relationship should be about helping others deal. Ignoring red flags will cost you later. You have got someone standing beside you that is stronger than the one standing against you (Joshua 1:5). You are made for a purpose (Ephesians 2:1). Be still (Psalm 46:10). He restored my soul (Psalm 23:3).

I declare: "I am healed: I will see unexpected blessings and spiritual insight."

NOVEMBER 5

Stay strong for your imperfect family. A family is not hindered by time, space, or circumstances. I did not have financial freedom, but I did have a close family, with family dinners, coffee, and desserts homemade by Mom. Sunday dinners were the best; the doorbell never stopped ringing. I did not know fashion designer names, but I knew all about family dedication. My dad especially valued our family time; it was the world to him. Do not look at what you do not have. Stay focused on the positive things you have learned from your parents. Nothing and no one is perfect. Celebrate the perfect moments that were invested in you and pass them down to your family. One day, you realize that material things mean nothing. All that matters is the well-being of the people in your life. Time spent is more valuable than money. A happy family is but an earlier heaven. We did not have it all together, but *together*, we had it all. Hatred nor jealousy are family values. Friends also became our chosen family. Every good and perfect gift is from above (James 1:17). The most wasted of all days is one without laughter. For this child, I have prayed for (1 Samuel 1:27). You are loved, little children. Let us not love with words or speech but with actions and in truth (1 John 3:18). Find your tribe and love them strong.

I declare: "I will be devout to my family with God's guidance."

NOVEMBER 6

Ask God to help you release whatever made you feel unwanted and unloved as a child. Declare: I am fearfully and wonderfully made by God. Most people do not try to understand you, so stop explaining or expecting. Let it go. Tell the truth even if you feel judged, invisible, humiliated, rejected, betrayed, and brokenhearted. You cannot make it in a fake, make-believe world. Never defend yourself. Often, the one who cries victim is the one who did the wrong. Happiness is lying down at night and realizing, through prayer, you broke a toxic cycle. Staying consistent in the Word will transform average into excellence. Your success for life, no matter the trial, is the sum of small efforts repeated from the Word day in and day out. People rationalize you are a bad person to diminish their ill-treatment of you. Be careful about one who mocks your values. Healthy relationships require give and take. You have access to the Wonderful Counselor who has a solution for you. Work through your issues, do not let them simmer. Respect others without letting them rule you. Do not get on the edge with others. Ask God to show you any walls in your relationships and ask Him to help tear them down with His love. But as for you, be strong and do not give up, for your work will be rewarded (2 Chronicles 15:7).

I declare: "I am fearfully and wonderfully made by God. I will seek His word daily."

NOVEMBER 7

There are some things you just cannot write a check for, like becoming the best version of yourself which needs your discipline. Read Ecclesiastes chapter 7. It is impossible for anyone to see you clearly while they are controlling you. Fear and worry are interest paid in advance on something you will never own. Still worrying? Insecure people make you feel insecure. Lying people accuse you of lying. Cheating people always accuse you of cheating. Pay attention. Follow the Word and the Holy Spirit, for they know the way and keep you balanced in the truth. Do not hold grudges. You will not embrace your destiny if you cannot let go of your history. It does not matter how old you are. Surround yourself with people you want to be like. Victory holds hands with conflict. The devil is looking for you in the history part, but God has moved you to a new season. Stay right there. You cannot go into the new with that old attitude. Never fear the haters, or that will bring you conflict. Forgiveness is empowering yourself. We must raise godly children in a broken world. Pay attention. Seek godly advice (Proverbs 19:20). Give thanks for answers (Psalm 28:7). Tune out distractions (Luke 5:16).

I declare: "For His name's sake, my sins are forgiven (pardoned through His name and on account of confessing His name). Call on Jesus."

NOVEMBER 8

Each day will present enough trouble of its own. No matter what, show your integrity. This is how others will trust you. Trust is the most important element fact for all relationships. You do not know people until you see them interact with a child or have a bad situation suddenly pop up. People with strong integrity will never have to worry about their conduct. It takes two to have a healthy relationship. This is for all relationships, not just marriage. The best reason to let go of toxic relationships is because your child is watching. A person who really values you would never risk wanting to lose you. It is the Lord who goes before you. He will be with you. He will not leave or forsake you. Do not fear (Deuteronomy 31:8). If I did anything right in my life, it was giving my heart to my children. In our house, we took second chances. We did it by grace. We did real. We did, "I am sorry." We did loud well. We do hugs. We do love. We do family. Marriage is an endless sleepover with your favorite person. Spouses are not called to think alike; we are called to think together. Our diversity created better decision-making for our future. Glory to God. It is not your job to fix people. We do not know what tomorrow holds; God is the timekeeper. Our times are in His hands (Psalm 31:15). Eyes forward. It is time to crush your goals.

I declare: "It is by free grace that I am saved, delivered from judgment, through my faith."

NOVEMBER 9

Truth serum! Tribulations produce perseverance. God is not the author of confusion or error.

> *For this very reason, make every effort to add to your faith goodness; and to goodness, knowledge; and to knowledge, self-control; and to self-control, perseverance; and to perseverance, godliness.*
>
> 2 Peter 1:5–6 (NIV)

The most challenging part of your journey in life is all about your perseverance! We all have differences and difficulties on our path in life. Are you a complainer? A whiner? Or are you easily fooled by distractions? It is your willingness to stay strong intentionally. It is written, "No eye has seen, no ear has heard, and no mind has imagined the things that God has prepared for those who love him" (1 Corinthians 2:9, ISV). His kingdom cannot be shaken. Worship and thanksgiving will change your perspective to keep you balanced. An emotional roller coaster attitude has got to go. Grumbling will set you way back, just do not do it. Let His presence put a fire in you. He will lead you the way you should go. Keep your total focus on Him. Stop the outside chatter. To avoid confusion, seek to please Him only, not others. That is a losing battle. Stay successful by seeking Him first and staying in communication with the King of kings. You cannot go wrong there. This will be a successful day. Do not focus or talk about your brokenness.

I declare: "I have the holy fire of God in me. I cannot fail."

NOVEMBER 10

Decide today what kind of life you want. Then say no to everything else. I know firsthand that extraordinary does not come from staying stuck in your comfort zone. Your dream written down with a date is your goal. Your goal, broken down, will become your steps. Your daily steps, which are your habits, will become your success. It is your daily routine that will make it happen. It is not magic. It is intentional, by choice, every day, every moment. Mind your own business and do what you need to do to change your life. Make it happen. I stopped venting! Then I started praying over my goals. I do not need sympathy, and neither do you. You need strength to set yourself apart and fearlessly move forward with your success. Success does not come from what you may do occasionally. You must be consistent daily with your goals. Stop negative self-talk. Stop abusing your body. Stop saying you can't do it. Stop medicating yourself, stop giving yourself away, stop hiding, and stop being insecure. I have been guilty of all the above. Get up. Rise up. Stop the tears and the fears. Start right now. Nobody is going to do this for you. You have got to do the hard work. You are valuable and so worth it. Stop thinking like a victim. That is a lie from the enemy to hold you down.

I declare: "I can do all things through Christ who strengthens me daily" (Philippians 4:13, NKJV).

NOVEMBER 11

Question? Are you feeding your faith, or are you feeding your fear? Stop feeding the fear with negativity and gossip. You must starve that deadly emotion of fear. Do not give into your fears because it is negative energy from the enemy to stop the plan of God in your life. You will always have faith and fear in your daily life. The one you entertain will stay. My daily routine starts right off with building up my faith. As soon as my feet hit the floor, I start confessing my favorite scriptures out loud. Right after that, I read several faith-filled devotional books with scriptures, which is a sword against the thoughts of the enemy. I pray, work out, then listen to several faith-filled messages while I get ready for the day. Now, I can launch my day in pure faith. This daily habit will stop the bad energy of fear. You cannot expect fear to just disappear. You have to go to spiritual awakening daily. It is warfare. You must focus on your faith. Whichever emotion you feed will stay. Are you with me on this goal setting of building your faith up stronger than ever before? This is the only reason why I am strong in the Lord. I work it! I am only a vessel like you. God is not the spirit of fear; He is of love, peace, and a sound mind (2 Timothy 1:7).

I declare: "The fear of man brings a snare, but because I lean on, trust in, and put my confidence in the Lord, I am safe and set up on high."

NOVEMBER 12

You have a pocket full of money, but you have no peace; you are still broke. Do not go broke staying in turmoil. Peace will always begin within. If you lack peace, your world will be chaotic. A fresh start is not a new place; it is a new mindset. Protect your peace, get rid of toxicity, cleanse your space, and cultivate agape love. That is unconditional love. Calm yourself first; then your storm will pass. Your whole life can become a masterpiece when you decide to master peace. You cannot make others happy, so stop trying. Peace is rewiring your brain to process life as it is, not what you think others are doing.

Peace is acceptance and giving up manipulation and control. I will breathe. Declare: For God is not the author of any confusion but of peace (1 Corinthians 14:33). I will not let my worry control me. I will not let stress break me. I will not quit. I declare: "I love a calm house. I love a calm life. Don't let evil conquer you but conquer evil by doing good (Romans 12:21)." Write your thoughts down. Your limit may be your thinking. Set goals, say prayers, and work hard. Champions train for life; losers complain and remain stuck. New habits, new life.

I declare: "I love a calm house. I love a calm life. I will not let evil conquer me. I will conquer evil by doing good."

NOVEMBER 13

No means next opportunity! You can create opportunities out of no. Stop overthinking it. You cannot keep replaying it either. Oh, do not feed that self-doubt. You deserve so much more. This is a test; I repeat, this is a test. I am surrounded by God's favor (Psalm 5:12). I have been through the fire and water, but you brought us out to a place of abundance (Psalm 66:12). Stop talking; stay humble. No finger-pointing allowed. You do not know the storm God has asked them to walk through. It has got to go. Your healing will start with your thought life and what you speak. Life and death are in the power of the tongue. This is all part of the process. This is your "for such a time as this moment." Yes, of course, I have changed. Pain does that to people. You have a choice to practice stress or practice peace. Never question who God removes from your life. I to myself, *I gotcha boo*. You are more likely to achieve your goals if you keep them to yourself. I walk like I got it because I know it is coming. That is faith. It does not matter who comes against you. Because the Lord will fight for you, you need to be still (Exodus 14:14). Perhaps this is the moment for which you have been created for (Esther 4:14).

I declare: "The Lord watches over His word to perform it."

NOVEMBER 14

Do not be so creative that you create new problems for yourself daily. I worry when I am trying to do everything myself. When I live in peace, it is because I do remember God is in control of everything, and I am not. Forgive yourself for not knowing better at the time you messed up. Being kind to yourself is the best medicine you will ever take. Healing too. Healing is the end of your inner battle; that is why it is so important to be kind to yourself daily. Work on you for you. There are parts of you that you do not even know yet; get excited. Your thinking runs or ruins your life. Gratitude is the vitamin for your soul man. Stay quiet; you have nothing to prove to anyone. Humility is growth and prepares you for the next level. Anger is a punishment we give to ourselves, do not go there; it is not worth it at all. Grow! Love yourself and listen to you. God is going to do something spectacular. Stay in peace. Life tip: Do you. Notice three things you are grateful for right now. And even the very hairs of your head are all numbered. So don't be afraid; you are worth more than many sparrows (Matthew 10:30–31).

I declare: "God can always point to me as an example of the incredible wealth of His favor and kindness toward me, as shown in all He has done for me through Christ Jesus."

NOVEMBER 15

Every person has potential, and only the Lord knows what it is! Be the best you! Beware: If the devil knows he can capture your thinking, then he knows he can stop you in your tracks and steal your victory. Greater is He who is in you than he who rules the world. The Holy Spirit reigns supreme in your life. He will show you the things of Christ. There is absolutely no match for how He can prepare you to stand against the enemy. He has done it for me, and I know He will do it for you. We need to put on the mind of Christ daily to stand against the wiles of the devil. It is so beautiful to have the spirit of the Lord upon you. Walk by faith and not by how you feel. Emotions can lead you down the wrong road. The power of the Holy Spirit prepares us for the day against the enemy. I would be a defeated foe if I did not prepare myself daily. Seek Him now, call out His name, be set free from unforgiveness, and be delivered from your strong-holds. There is salvation, redemption, healing, and forgiveness in His name. Do not stay in a dry place. The water represents the power of the Holy Spirit. It is fresh and washes you clean. It has a powerful force. We are made up of 90 percent water. We need daily replenishing so we do not become bitter, cloudy, or stale. The Holy Spirit will shine the light on every dark place so you do not spoil your life. Cry out today.

I declare: "I find wisdom, and I find life and receive favor from the Lord."

NOVEMBER 16

Self-control is doing God's will, not your own. Be real. Be kind. Love always. "Blessed are the pure in heart, for they shall see God" Matthew 5:8, NKJV). The Lord does not care how many Bible verses you memorize but how you treat people. If you are a beautiful face and are mean to others, you have an ugly heart. If you claim to have faith but do not control your tongue, your relationships are worthless. If you pray well in public and maintain a holy appearance, but your behavior reveals otherwise, you are fooling yourself. I have learned what not to do. Life was not easy, and I needed God to help me through. Do not be blind to your faults and quick to judge others for the wrong you are doing. It does not pay to be the critic or the judge. Sometimes, people who are tired of the drama are the ones causing it. I seek the Lord first daily to stay fair, be in check with the Holy Spirit, and be salt and light. Your character shows through your actions, not where you sit on Sunday! A grateful heart is a magnet for miracles. Let your gentleness be evident to all (Philippians 4:5). Open my eyes to see the wonderful truths of your instructions (Psalm 119:18). Life is a miracle, and every breath we take is a gift from God.

I declare: "Christ is seated in heavenly places, and I am seated in Him. He is above all principalities and powers, and all things are under His feet."

NOVEMBER 17

When God has selected you, it does not matter who else has rejected you. That was my story. If you have adversity in your life, it is because God wants to use you! Many ministries have been started because others long to share the discomfort of what has happened to them and encourage others that are going through similar situations. There is a common thread known by those who have suffered and lived out the same difficulties. A zillion things can go wrong in life; you also can receive unexpected blessings along that path through powerful prayer. This is exactly how I started *I Am Just a Vessel* by writing about my hard times to the Lord in a journal. I would not change a thing! Remember, growing might feel like breaking at first. Do not let your age keep you from looking your best. You were not made to give up. Goodbye, comfort zones, doubt, and fear. Hello, opportunity, new beginnings, and supernatural power in Jesus. You are going to be telling a different story very soon. Keep seeking God. The clean-hearted will always win in the end. God can restore what is broken and change it into something amazing. All you need is faith (Joel 2:25).

I declare: "I call out to High God, the God who holds me together. He sends orders from heaven and saves me. God delivers generous love; He makes good on His word."

NOVEMBER 18

What is the best way to improve the growing quality of your relationships? Admit when you are wrong humbly, and zip it when you are right! Real simple. When being ignored by one who means the most to you, the reaction in your brain is very similar to physical pain. Unexpressed emotions never die. They are buried and come forth later in ugly ways. When you meet someone, always ask God to reveal their true self and their intentions and, of course, their true character. Pray for this year to be a year of increased discernment. Anyone who stops learning is old, whether they are twenty or eighty. Keep on learning to help you stay young. The most amazing and powerful thing is to keep your mind fresh, young, and learning. Declare: This is my last year of tolerating anything less than I deserve. Thank you for all the lessons. I am ready for the new. Relationships last longer when you do not tell people about your business. Staying silent is golden. Focus on change. You are God's masterpiece (Ephesians 2:10). You are more precious than rubies (Proverbs 3:15). Nothing is impossible with God (Luke 1:37). Encourage one another (1 Thessalonians 5:11).

I declare: "This is my last year of tolerating anything less than I deserve."

NOVEMBER 19

Do not let the ugly in others destroy the beautiful in you. You are crazy to everyone who cannot control you. Cancel that pity party, pull yourself together, and take responsibility for every thought. Do not sink into waves of panic. Declare: "Teach me not to rely on my own strength but to always rely on You (Proverbs 3:5). Help me pull back from my routine to focus on what's important" (Romans 12:2).

A good person will want you to shine. They want you to be your amazing self. Often others who criticize your life are the same people that do not know the price you have paid to get to where you are today. Celebrate anyway. Be around others who are proud to have you. How others treat you is how they feel about you. Period. Pay attention. If you live for the approval of others, you will suffer from their rejection. Do not go there. Do not lose yourself. Home is the nicest word there is. Always feel at home with yourself. Make new decisions. I talked to God daily, and that is what has made me powerful. Kneel before God so you can stand before anyone (Romans 8:31). Whatever you are thinking, think *bigger*. "[...] Be our [my] strength every morning..." (Isaiah 33:2b, NIV) He heals the wounds of every shattered heart (Psalm 147:3).

I declare: "Teach me not to rely on my own strength but to always rely on You."

NOVEMBER 20

You do not have to perform for God to love you; thankfulness, gratitude, and trust are all you need to keep yourself open to His radiant love. The trust is in Him, not yourself. Right now, receive His unconditional love. A huge trick of the enemy to keep you down is when you feel like you do not measure up to your expectations. Be aware. You can make predictions for your future, but that is a part of your imagination. Only God knows the future. Stay in the present and live today to the fullest without groaning about it. Encourage yourself in the Lord and ask the Holy Spirit to help you with this one day. Then repeat it tomorrow. God has heard all about what you are going through; nothing is unique to God. The enemy wants you to feel like your life will be defeated. Do not listen to the lies of the enemy. Go to God, confess your fear, and keep it at His feet. Do not pick it up again; leave it there. Declare: I trust God to do the impossible and put me on the path to victory. I have no peace or power to face this army that is attacking me. I do know what to do, but to keep my eyes on Him (2 Chronicles 20:12). Trust Him regardless of that situation.

I declare: "I trust God to do the impossible and put me on the path to victory."

NOVEMBER 21

Staying mentally focused on good things is how you develop wisdom. You do not always have to tell your side of the story; time will. God knows, and that is simply enough. Life will teach you that you are not in control of anything. The only One that can truly satisfy the human heart is the One that made it. Your attitude is the little thing that will make a huge difference. Humility is not thinking less of yourself. It is thinking of yourself less. With age comes an inner strength from the Holy Spirit of not being overly concerned of what others think. God only knows what you have really been through. Honesty saves everyone's time. It does not matter how educated, financially secure, fashionable, how cool you think you are, or what title you hold; it is how you treat others that ultimately tells it all. Every one of us has scars. You will not defeat the demons you enjoy playing with. "The Lord is with you, mighty warrior" (Judges 6:12b, NIV). Long before the enemy targeted you, God knew you and chose you. Your growth is beautiful. Just keep getting better. You know yourself better than anyone. Do not let others make you think it is all in your head. Wake up every morning and speak to yourself, "I can do all things through Christ who strengthens me; I can do this."

I declare: "Pride lands me flat on my face, but humility prepares me for honor."

NOVEMBER 22

You can bet distractions are a set up from the enemy to stop you right in your tracks for a huge setback. Be aware they are not from God. This is when you need to zipper up your mouth. Do not repay evil for evil. Do not retaliate with insults even if others insult you. Instead, pay them back with a blessing! For this is what God has called you to do, and He will bless you for it (1 Peter 3:9). This is the highest form of spiritual maturity. It is being obedient to the Word. One of the greatest indicators of your spiritual maturity is shown in how you respond to the offensive attitudes of others. We must be more God-conscious and less self-conscious. Maturity is for His ministry. Maturity is walking away from that drama and others who threaten your value and peace. Patience is when you can be mad, but you choose to rise above it. In my good times and my bad times, I will trust the plan of God. Maturity is not your age. It simply means using manners, telling the truth, being sensitive to others, and how you react. As iron sharpens iron, so a friend sharpens a friend (Proverbs 27:17). Talk to God before you get in the trap of overthinking. Be transformed by the renewal of your mind. That's spiritual maturity. Know your worth.

I declare: "The Lord loves those who love Him, and those who seek Him early and diligently shall find Him."

NOVEMBER 23

We become what we think. If we think confusion, we become confused. If we think godly wisdom from His holy Word, we become wise and holy and one with Him. The devil tries to pull you through the thoughts of your mind so he can take advantage of you. He will make you delirious. Stay constantly filled with the Holy Spirit and give no place to the evil one. Do not be conformed or concerned with this world. Be transformed by the daily renewing of your mind, that you may prove what is good of God and acceptable and His perfect will for your life (Romans 12:2). The spirit of love will never fail you. The more you fixate on the negative: fault finding, finger-pointing, and evil speaking, the more power you give to the negative force. You have the mind of the Messiah, so use it. Renewing your mind brings health and happiness. It will rewire your brain for comfort. Push back the darkness with renewed positive thinking from God's word for complete wholeness. Your thinking carries authority from the Holy Spirit with the Word. Stinking thinking is pointless and poisonous. It brings sickness to your body. Only you can stop toxic thinking. Happiness and health come from your brain, not what you eat or drink. Switch on your brain for optimal health and wellness. You are what you think! If God is for you, then who can be against you (Romans 8:31)?

I declare: "I ask and receive, and my joy is made full."

NOVEMBER 24

Broken? Knocked down? Defeated? Do you have pain that most could not handle? Look fear in the eye. Do not run and hide; remain standing on the Word, and believe these battles belong to God. Do what God shows you to do. Be a spiritual warrior! You are unbelievable according to His Word. Everything you are going through and went through prepares you for what the Lord has told you! When people hurt you over and over, they become the sandpaper in life. The scratches may hurt a while, polishing and preparing you to be used for His glory. This is called transformation. One morning you wake up and realize you are done with things that do not bring you peace. Get the key out of others' pockets to your life and start living. Break the cycle. Do not beg for attention. What lies behind us has passed and is gone. What lies before us is so much greater. What lies within us is supernatural. Shine among those who never believed you could. Stay taking care of yourself. You will look better, feel better, act better, and attract better. It all starts with you. Rise up, take courage, and do it (Ezra 10:4). I have struggled, cried, and almost gave up. I learned. I prayed. I tried. I hoped. I got up. And I do it again daily. Blessed are those who believe without seeing (John 20:29).

I declare: "I welcome change and strive to become who I was created to be. I am so blessed."

NOVEMBER 25

Being beautiful and handsome is being comfortable in your own skin. I said a prayer for you that God would touch you with His healing hand and give you the strength you need to get through. He is at my right hand; I shall not be shaken (Psalm 16:8). "You make everything beautiful in its time" (Ecclesiastes 3:11). What the enemy means for evil, God intended for good. Put your trust in Him. In a world full of trends, remain classic, heartfelt, and just plain real. Do not use your freedom as an excuse to do bad things. Do you feel like life is impossible? God chose you before the foundation of this earth. God is still the best doctor, and prayer is still the best medicine. Prayer is so powerful. You are prepared for the inevitable; you have nothing to fear. God loves us all equally, and we know all things work together for good to those who love God and trust Him. Guard your own words, for they have power. You cannot curse, speak doubt, speak negatively over yourself, and expect a miracle. Once you have prayed, praise and thank God for what you just asked Him to do. You must stop speaking defeat, failure, and just plain evil stuff that will not work. That allows the enemy to slip back in. Zipper up.

I declare: "Lord, I bring to You my burdens and situations. I cannot make it without Your help. When prayer becomes my habit, miracles will become my lifestyle."

NOVEMBER 26

The most powerful single ingredient in the secret formula of success is having great people skills. Stay in practice of seeking God first, or fear sets in and creates phobias. Ask God daily, "Preserve me, Lord" (Psalm 16:1). God will establish boundaries around you daily if you ask! Are you practicing daily for that protective hedge (Psalm 91:11)? Or are you soaring into toxic thinking, which is the norm? Toxic thinking stops your ability to sort out your emotions. Put all bitterness, rage, yelling, blasphemy, and wickedness far away from you (Ephesians 4:31). Joy and happiness cease when you focus on memories. When you get stuck in negative thinking, you cannot deal with your emotions. Then they turn deadly. Overacting and overthinking will kick it up a notch. This is how flight mode happens, and it wars against your body. Bad thoughts are harmful. Thinking carries authority over our lives because we can customize it daily. Be aware of your thinking. Do not let anyone or anything steal your joy. Rejoice always and in everything give thanks; for that is God's will for you in Christ Jesus. Giving thanks! Learn to trust God for all He is and all He can give. You need the teacher, who is the Holy Spirit, which is love.

I declare: "I will live a balanced life."

NOVEMBER 27

Hold on! I need to overthink this again! Never lose your sparkle. If speaking kindly to plants helps them grow, imagine what speaking kindly to humans can do. Go everywhere today and be awesome. "I once was lost, but now I am found" ("Amazing Grace"). Do not argue. Be okay and go about your life. Your brain has a delete button. Listening to faith-filled sermons daily brings about a great mood change and has a positive effect on your health. There is healing in God's Word. Stop negative thinking. Life is hard. People are selfish, and people change, but life is also beautiful. We must have complete faith in God's ability to move mountains in our lives. There is power in persistent prayer (Micah 7:7). "God, I pray for protection from anything that was not sent by You, in Jesus' name." Be still (Exodus 14:14)! Surround yourself with laughter. Be patient. God blesses those who patiently endure the testing and temptation (James 1:12). God will provide (Philippians 4:19). Your health is an investment. Happiness is peace of mind. We pick what we plant in everyday life. What makes you different has also made you beautiful. Your smile is the best makeup you could ever wear. Grateful. Thankful. Blessed. Be kind or stay quiet.

I declare: "Lord, I will sleep in peace tonight, for You are bigger than anything and already have a plan."

NOVEMBER 28

Family jewels! Celebrate one another. Grateful and thankful. God first! In every area of marriage, my spouse is my partner, not my problem. Together, we win and lose. Vow to love. Anything meant to tear apart will strengthen when the head of your marriage is God. Together as a team, your foundation is indestructible, built upon the rock of the word. Make your marriage the safest place on earth. God is on your side. A great marriage is not found; it is built and maintained. Stop saying it is just a piece of paper. So is money, and you still work hard for it daily. Happy ever after is not a fairy tale; it is intentional work. Date your wife and flirt with your husband. Make your marriage more awesome than the memory of your wedding. Don't just tie the knot; keep the knot tied tight. No loose ends. Value and build each other up. We are two imperfect people serving a perfect God. Boundaries are the lock and key to a healthy relationship. Together, you can build a life you love. Keep God in the center. A husband is a leader with a heart of a servant, loving his wife gently. The most beautiful thing a woman wears is confidence. Marriage cannot thrive on leftover attention. In marriage, if both of you were alike, one of you would be unnecessary. Happily ever after starts with you!

I declare: "I am an excellent wife, the crown of my husband."

NOVEMBER 29

Do not be fooled by outward glamour; the state of one's soul determines beauty. Protect your mind from thought curses or a holier-than-thou attitude. The humble will seek their God at work and be glad. Let all who seek God's help be encouraged today (Psalm 69:32). Let rejection fuel you, not break you. Be comfortable if others don't see your true worth. The most important thing in life is to find out your purpose for what God designed you to do for Him. Working for God will last from here to eternity. Walk like you know your God-given purpose. Elegance is the only beauty that remains in style. Real women help other women. Do you fix another woman's crown without telling the world it was crooked? Strong women build other women up instead of holding or tearing them down. Empowering women empowers women. She celebrates, she smiles, she's kind, she knows health, she makes time for herself, she understands difficulties and moves on quickly. You are amazing. Gentlemen are attracted to ladies. It is a man's job to respect women, but it is a women's job to be someone to respect. Bring the joy together. A wise man once said nothing. Be that type of gentleman you would handpick for your daughter. Struggle attracts the female you need. A gentleman only has eyes for his lady.

I declare: "Integrity and uprightness preserve me, for I wait for and expect the Lord."

NOVEMBER 30

Live your best life! You do not need to understand everything to be a vessel for God. Question marks in your brain stretch your faith to grow in Him. Unanswered questions will instantly crucify your flesh to the bottom of that cross to stop reasoning and throw your hands up in the air and really trust God. You say you trust God, but do you? When you trust God, your thinking will enter in a place of total rest and relaxation. God will let you have understanding on several issues but not everything. This is when you need to be obedient to His Word. Stop talking about issues you are trying to figure out. You will wear yourself out. From this time forth forever, "Praise the Lord!" (Psalm 115:18b, NKJV) Through your gratitude, destructive ways of your discontentment will close. Stop waiting for the perfect setup. Decide to enjoy the gift of life today. Life goes by regardless of how you choose to think. Thanksgiving destroys discontentment. Refuse to complain; it is ugly to your soul and body. Renew your mind and fix it on Him. Stop with the "should a...,could a..., or would a...." We can stress anytime. But today is the day to rejoice and be glad (Psalm 118:24). Winning the battle in my mind. Forget the "I will be so happy when I..." because it is a huge lie from the enemy. Be happy because you get to live this one day.

I declare: "I choose to rejoice in this day and stay in peace."

December

For, "Whoever would love life and see good days must keep their tongue from evil and their lips from deceitful speech."
1 Peter 3:10 (NIV)

Your words are powerful. Be careful what you speak.

DECEMBER 1

"Set your minds on things above, not on earthly things" (Colossians 3:2, NIV). Whether you remain stuck or train harder to approach your goals, the next few months will go by. Creative thinking damages your breaking point. Write your thoughts down, then beside your thoughts, put God's thoughts. If you want a Superman, you must be a Wonder Woman of the Word. Honor God in all that you do. Keep quiet if you are not minding your own business, do not have facts, are going to offend a weaker believer, will damage a reputation, cannot speak without yelling, or will be ashamed of your words later (Proverbs 14:10). Blaming the one you hurt is fake repentance. It is not a fib. It is not gossip. Now, truth is the new hate speech. God never commanded you to trust people; He commanded you to love all people and trust Him. This is the Word of God. We must be careful not to become a modern-day Jezebel. They love God, and their god is their selves. The Jezebel spirit is going to gain power through intimidation, fear, manipulation, threats, and other ways that are, of course, not from God. Stay away from pride and arrogance. These are born out of witchcraft and rebellion. Your greatest weapon in spiritual warfare is the Word of God. By their fruits, you will know them (Matthew 7:15–16a).

I declare: "Soft answers turn away wrath, but grievous words stir up anger."

DECEMBER 2

We know that all things work together for the good, for God so loved the world. Trust in God right now with all your heart. Keep your mind sound and disciplined. Your cup is about to run over with blessings you did not see coming! Your answer is always in your praise! Exercising is a blessing, not a chore. The real workout starts when you always feel like quitting, physically and spiritually. Establish a morning routine by a scheduled time. Avoid complaining, gossiping, envying, doubting, fearing, and judging. Successful people read, spend time encouraging their family members, exercise, pursue their passions, eat well, sleep earlier, learn new things, and disconnect to spend time alone. Decluttering is a huge plus in all areas. Plan your day first thing. Smile at yourself in the mirror. Hug others with your whole heart. Waste of time: creating fake problems so you do not have to deal with the real. Stay inspired. Pray on it. Pray over it. Pray through it all. Our job is to truly love others, not to truly judge others. When friends try to help us figure things out, their own flaws and sinfulness can also get in the way. Only God understands you perfectly; go straight to Him. He counts the stars and calls them all by name (Psalm 147:4). God will bring you through the fire (Psalm 66:12).

I declare: "God will bring me through the fire."

DECEMBER 3

This is the season things are just coming together for you, even if you get a "suddenly unexpected something." The Lord is greater than anything that just pops up. And then...God stepped in. What God is about to do, no man can stop because you are kind to everyone and hospitable to all. God is going to bless you. God's timing is perfect. God is the waymaker. He is the designer of your future. God has chosen you to make you a blessing to many. Do you take in consideration what others are really doing in life? You fall in love with people who make you love the person you are when you are around them. How they treat you is how they feel about you. Pray and declare: I quit overthinking and feeding self-doubt. It is funny how dead people receive more flowers than living ones. Regret is stronger than gratitude. Give others time. Do not be the same. Be better. God loves you now as you are, imperfect. Do not set resolutions; rather, set up intentions. Not me, but the grace of God within me. God is faithful even when we are faithless (Psalm 106:43). God's plans will always be greater and more beautiful than your disappointments. "Deliver me, Lord!"

I declare: "I quit overthinking and feeding self-doubt."

DECEMBER 4

Everything depends upon believing in God. Do not rest on your feelings. Take a break from your thoughts. Positive people do not let those nasty thoughts grow and destroy them or others. Pray about your healing and believe you can receive it, not because you are good but because God loves you. Know your worth. Remember, He died for every ounce of you. Others say you are important to them, yet make you feel unimportant. Don't consent to those feelings. Expectations can hurt you. The worst is getting hurt by the one you explained your pain to. Pray. God has a plan. Strength comes from overcoming obstacles, possible through Christ. Make broken look beautiful. When you stand before God at the end of this life, I pray that you can say you used every bit of your gift that He blessed you with. I am sorry if someone you loved made you think it was hard to love you. That rock bottom became my solid friend, which I rebuilt my life on when I realized God died for me, giving me abundant life. He loves us no matter what. Do not listen to others' rude remarks or backhanded compliments; that is what they really feel about themselves. No one warns you about the amount of mourning in growth. Surround yourself with beautiful images of your God-given vision.

I declare: "Even when I do not understand, I will praise You, Lord." I know the Lord is always with me; I will not be shaken (Psalm 16:8–9).

DECEMBER 5

Just wait until you see why you are going through this trial right now. What God is doing behind the scenes is beyond what you are praying for. It will work out for everyone involved. The Lord rains on the just and the unjust. You may see difficulties, but you will not be defeated. For this battle is not yours, stop trying to fix it. The battle belongs to God (2 Chronicles 20:15). Self is the worst enemy a Christian has. Do not stop praying because you do not feel like it. Stress creates a sense of urgency. Faith reassures you that it will happen when God wants it to. His timing is perfect. If you are living right, you will never have to hide anything. The motto "be yourself" is counterfeit to God's Word, "Be holy, for I am holy" (1 Peter 1:16b, NKJV). This is what we need to be! We may blame circumstances, but going back to past mistakes begins in the heart. This is a trick from the enemy to trap you. Human unbelief cannot alter the character of our God. Be intimate with God daily, and you will not be intimidated by anyone. Imperfect and unworthy, yet saved by His grace. In the last days, good will be called evil, and evil called good (Isaiah 5:20). I will go before you and make the crooked places straight (Isaiah 45:2).

I declare: "I am growing and becoming strong in spirit, filled with wisdom, and the grace of God is upon me."

DECEMBER 6

Be that type of kindness, no matter where you go, that you add value to the spaces and lives around you. I pray that you heal from the things no one ever apologized for. Wanting to be treated well is not being selfish. God has no phone, but I talk to Him first thing every day. He has no Facebook, yet He remains my best friend. He does not tweet, but I always follow Him. Work at living in peace with everyone (Hebrews 12:14). Others may not thank you, applaud you, or give you deserving credit. But be assured, heaven commends those who serve others.

This life is about discovering who God created you to be for His purpose on earth, not about finding yourself for just you. Do not get distracted from what God has already told you to do. Refuse to let the world corrupt you (James 1:27). If you are not hungry for God, you may be too full of yourself. Prayer is the cure for the confused mind, the weary soul, and the broken heart. Do not get tangled up in emotional roller coasters; bow and flee right now. Emotions cannot be your decision-maker. Bad company ruins good morals (1 Corinthians 15:33). Pray first and then make plans. Do not plan, and then pray for your plan to work. Get rid of bitterness, rage, anger, harsh words, and evil. Be tender-hearted and forgiving (Ephesians 4:31–32).

I declare: "I will listen to and obey God."

DECEMBER 7

If you only knew the value of this trial! He knew you before He put you in your mother's womb; everything orchestrated before we know or understand it. He is God and holds the keys to life and death. When you do not see a way out, when all you hear is the doctor's report, when your mate does not see things your way.... God has a plan. This is when you kneel, pray, and seek the face of God for your answers. I believe the report of the Lord. I believe in open heavens and opened doors by faith. Praise the Lord in still situations. Focus your mind on the Holy Spirit, and you will have life and peace (Romans 8:5–6). Your mind is powerful and incredible. So, what are you thinking? Only God knows the future; what you do not know. Trust Him. Do not let your heart stray from God's Word. Allow the Lord to live through you. I pray that I have the DNA of the Holy Spirit daily. I cannot change myself, and neither can you. "I do not want to miss all that You have planned for me. I turn every fear, sorrow, distraction, and disappointment over to You today. I believe You will use all of them for Your glory. I turn over every hurt to You. I have freedom in You. When I feel overwhelmed, I turn right to You. You have everything under Your control. Hallelujah."

I declare: "I need firm boundaries from You, Lord. I crave to walk in Your wisdom and not my own."

DECEMBER 8

Do not let hard days win. Wake up with a victory attitude, "I can't wait to see what God is going to do today." Dress like you have already won, and it is the best day of your life. Every day is very special. Be picky with your clothing, friends, time, character, intelligence, strength, and style. They make you unique, and that creates your beauty. Ten years from now, you want to say you chose your lifestyle. Make sure you do not see yourself through the eyes of one who does not value you. Know your beautiful worth. Fashion is the armor to survive the reality of everyday life. The Word of God is our primary weapon against the deception of the enemy. In the midst of a spiritual attack, clothe yourself in the full armor of God. The days are evil; dress appropriately (Ephesians chapter 6). The armor of God dresses you for true success. Preach with your lifestyle before you preach with your mouth. Transform from a worrier to a warrior. Be empowered on earth. Show up and suit up. The Lord will conquer (Deuteronomy 28:7). Put on the whole armor of God to stand against the wiles of the devil.

I declare: "As I dwell in the secret place of the Highest, I shall abide and say of the Lord, 'He is my refuge and my fortress. My God, in Him I will trust.'"

DECEMBER 9

God is moving you. Stop shrinking yourself to fit in others' opinions that you have outgrown. Stay with the winners. We cannot judge others from the choices they have made. We do not know the options they had to choose from. Others who do not live life will try to stop you from living yours. You can start late, look different, be uncertain, and be extremely successful. You cannot be a prisoner of your past. That has to flee, and you need to get set free in Jesus. Those generational curses can keep you trapped. Be aware, through the Word of God, Satan loves to take what is beautiful and ruin it. God takes what is ruined and makes it beautiful again. Be aware: emotions cannot be your decision-maker. Stop and pray. In His precious presence, everything changes. Stay in prayer. Prayer is the best medicine. He will fight your battles; stay silent. He will make a way for you; stop trying to do it on your own. The key is to trust His timing. Stay in fervent prayer. Declare: I am not in control, but I am deeply loved by the One who is. What a pity that we plan only things that we can do by ourselves. God is looking for those He can do the impossible with! Do not shine so others can see you. *Shine* so that others can see Him in you. "[...] Speak, Lord, for your servant is listening..." (1 Samuel 3:9b, NIV)

I declare: "I am not in control, but I am deeply loved by the one who is."

DECEMBER 10

As human beings, you have free will. You can create good or evil with your choices. God has given us that power (Matthew 4:10). Your mind is powerful. You build others up because you know what it is like to be put down. Declare: A lot of things broke my heart, but it sure fixed my vision. What a beautiful feeling it is to be able to stand tall and declare: I fell apart several times, and it hurt for a moment, but I know God is in control, and I survived. "You are the Potter, and I am the clay; have Your way and work on me." Losing a relationship may hurt. But losing yourself in that relationship hurts longer. Though it hurts for a moment, let Him work on you. A lot of things broke my heart, but I can see so much better now. I know your story can be filled with brokenness, unfair treatment, and not being accepted. But I do know this for sure, Jesus saves; you have a peace in your soul and grace in your heart that has saved your life. What does the Bible say? "Let all that you do be done with love" (1 Corinthians 16:14, NKJV). You are God's masterpiece (Ephesians 2:10). Whenever you feel unloved, unimportant, or insecure, remember who you belong to (Ephesians 2:19–22). Love them anyway (Luke 23:34). You are exactly where God wants you to be.

I declare: "What broke my heart sure fixed my vision."

DECEMBER 11

Things get better with time. Hurry is not the nature of God. It is our nature to hurry. Speak to your children as if they were the most beautiful people on earth. Those who criticize the most sometimes do the least. I choose this day to walk in total forgiveness. No need to stress or worry; I must believe God is in control. Wake up. We are all busy. We all must decide to make our Holy Spirit fitness a priority. Pause for a second and realize how fortunate we are to be able to eat healthy, exercise, and run our day. And remember there is always room for improvement. Not everything has to be perfect to still be wonderful. We do not stop living because we grow old, we grow old because we just stop doing things. Your speed does not matter, forward is forward. The best thing I ever did was believe in myself. I am sorry for not believing in the confidence in God. He has always proven me wrong. Keep putting into practice all you learned and received from Him (Philippians 4:9). When you keep criticizing your kids, they do not stop loving you. They stop loving themselves. Your thought life is directly related to your own attitude. Think about that.

I declare: "Hope never disappoints or deludes or shames me, for God's love has been poured out in my heart through the Holy Spirit who has been given to me."

DECEMBER 12

A life rooted in God will stand firm (Proverbs 12:3). "I trust You, Lord, as my Waymaker and Healer." Command every damaged cell in your body to be repaired in the mighty name of Jesus. No weapon. I desire blessings that are not in disguise. My help comes from God (Psalm 121:2). "Your direction, Lord, is more important than speed." I believe our lives are getting ready for positive change. One of the best goodnight texts is, "I am praying for you." Do not stay in fear. I embraced pain as my gift of growth and motivation for change. Your body is a strong machine, but it must be fueled by your mind. It does not matter what you did yesterday, good or bad. Today is a new day; make it happen and change what you need to change. Believe you were born to achieve wonderful things. Complaining is weakness. Keep the negativity out of your life; it will drag you down. Cling to what is good (Romans 12:4). For we are God's masterpiece (Ephesians 2:10). Joy is power. Make each word a gift to someone. Every good and perfect gift is from above (James 1:17). God has you in the palm of His hand (Isaiah 49:16). Let go of the past. Stay grateful for what remains. Love is kind. I found peace.

I declare: "I command every damaged cell in my body to be repaired right now in the mighty name of Jesus."

DECEMBER 13

Do not get all wrapped up in getting ready for Christmas.

The reason for Christmas is way better than all the gorgeous wrappings. Our truth is Christ. Every Christmas has been all about you and me. He loved us so much that He came to earth in flesh to relate to us. It is the celebration of what Jesus did for us. Let's plan to have a beautiful, sweet, and savoring Christmas, praising Him and seeking Him about all for our new year. I am rededicating my ways, my words, and my heart to all of Him. He came to earth, He died for us, and He rose again to give you and me eternal life. The celebration of Him shall begin with all the lights, bows, wreaths, and beautiful wrappings. What about your Christmas? Do not get caught up in the gift-giving if you cannot do it. Give of yourself, your time, and your love. Give the gift that keeps on giving all year round. Tell someone all about your King. What a beautiful Christmas story for you to share, all about how He changed you for life. That is why we should celebrate Christmas. Let's currently shut down for Holy Spirit maintenance. He humbled Himself (Philippians 2:8). We were created in His image. Our families depend on this for their lives.

I declare: "The Lord is good to everyone, and His tender mercies are over all His works."

DECEMBER 14

The very breath of God is in you (Job 33:4). Your only limit is your defeated desires. God has something great in your future (Isaiah 43:19). The wrong people will always teach you the right life lessons. Honor God with a spirit of excellence. Always believe in yourself. Never ever hold on to anything tighter than you are holding on to God. No time for distractions or meddling in other people's business. Stop worrying (Matthew 6:34). Rejection? It is the test to see if you are serious about your dreams. Life! No one has ever become successful in the past. Leave it behind you. I hope manners are the next cool thing. Life rooted in God always stands firm. Grow where you are planted. At the end of every day, you only have yourself. Learn today to be your own best friend. No shortcuts. No quick fixes. No blaming others. No "I'll do tomorrow." No excuses. I have tried all of that. It makes you feel like a failure. If you do not value your time, neither will others. If someone locked you up in prison today and you lost all your freedom, would that situation you have right now be stopping you from living? Think about that for a moment. Live your life to the fullest. Pray. It causes miracles.

I declare: "I will always honor God with a spirit of excellence."

DECEMBER 15

By His wounds, we became healed (Isaiah 53:5). Keep praying. Have you ever felt so broken that when the right someone came in your life, it made you forget that another person even existed? Something that ran in your family for generations is coming to an end with you. What satan stole is about to be restored by God. Believe in miracles because you are one. It is all handled. Instead of getting defensive, just say, "Thanks for letting me know your thoughts." I will consider them. Not saying anything is always the best answer. Stay tactful. It is an art of making your point without making an enemy. How a person treats their family says a lot about their character. You know you cannot trust your tongue when you have bitterness in your heart. Shush until you heal. If you are not helping to make it right, then stop complaining about how wrong it is. End this sad story. Take nothing personally. Anger is a common expression of grief. All things are possible if you only believe (Mark 9:23). Our real help comes from the Lord, the Maker of heaven and earth (Psalm 124:8). It is your due season for an uncommon blessing. I am going to see the victory, for the battle belongs to the Lord.

I declare: "I am assured and know that (God being a partner in my labor) all things work together and are (fitting into a plan) for good to and for me because I love God and I am called according to (His) design and purpose."

DECEMBER 16

No matter what you face, the Lord is with you. Prayers are the key in the morning to open your day and the lock at night. "Thank You, God, for closing doors I wasn't strong enough to close." Do not complain; just ask God. With faith the size of a mustard seed, nothing is impossible (Matthew 17:20). Pain and grief change you. Stop breaking yourself down. Choose to survive. Worry ends when faith kicks in. You will overcome what you have been dealing with by faith. Do not be afraid to start something new by faith. The hard part about losing someone is learning to live without them by faith. To my younger self, "I am sorry for what you went through; I believed you were unworthy. I was not ready for you to leave. I was a teenage daughter survivor. I did not beg, force, or chase. I prayed, worked, and had faith. My life changed. I don't need you to believe in me; I need to believe in myself." If you are having trouble or struggling with thoughts of self-harm, you are not alone. Seek help immediately. What's up, beautiful?

Stay strong, mister! God can carry you through all storms. He did it for me; I know He will for you. Truly, God is my mighty rock and salvation (Psalm 62:6–8). We may not understand God's reason for allowing things to happen, but we must trust Him.

I declare: "My faith rests in the power of God, not in the wisdom of men."

DECEMBER 17

You have the power to build up or tear apart! Do not resist showing love to others. Your words need to be filled with love; this can and will heal you and those around you. Proven fact! Anxiety may be difficult to stop or manage. Reading the Word of God will filter and purify your mind. Say your verses out loud to keep your thinking clean. Haughtiness is not from God. We can't ignore our problems. We can keep all our problems in perspective by staying pure in our thoughts by reading His Word. Rejoice always in the Lord for a peaceful mind. Walk in peace. Treat everyone as if they were the most important person on the planet. Meditate on these things: Truth, nobility, things that are pure, of course, loveliness, and share things of a good report. Do not bear bad news, haughtiness, or things that are just plain rude. It is not from God. Even if you can quote scriptures, your actions and words to all must remain pure-hearted. Meditate on things that are praiseworthy. God has the final say. Trust Him; He works all things out for the good of all of us. He is mighty in battle. Walk in love. Only love has the power to heal. If we treat each other with love, we can alleviate mental and physical pain. Read Matthew 4:23.

I declare: "I rejoice for a peaceful mind; I walk in peace."

DECEMBER 18

Train them, "I quit," out of you. Win the battle in your mind and build your lifestyle. Good and bad habits are both addictive. Food is the most abused anxiety drug. Exercise is the most underutilized antidepressant. Running slowly in life is not a character flaw; quitting is. I am addicted to bettering myself. Whatever you do, give it 100 percent. Just keep showing up when most people quit. People lose their way when they lose their why. Attitude is that little thing that makes a huge difference. Be responsible. A lying person can't handle an honest one. Your mind is like your bed; you must make it up every day. Be careful who you let in. If your faith is not challenging you, it is not challenging evil. The most dangerous heart disease is a strong memory. Encourage others. I want someone to look at me and say, "Because of the Jesus in you, I could not or did not quit life." Be happy without reason, and you will be happy every season. Life! Treat people better than you are treated. Learn to see negative experiences as powerful, growing lessons. The first thing you should know about others is they are not you. Grateful is where I am at.

I declare: "I was not made to quit my responsibilities."

DECEMBER 19

I know God has a plan. Satan will try to target your mind. His weapon: lies. His purpose is to keep you ignorant of God's will. Your defense is "the inspired Word of God!" Speak like you love yourself. You have never lived one moment unloved. Let the one who created you define you, not your neighbor, not the co-worker, and not the salesperson. Some people cannot function without being negative. Why? Bringing others down so they may feel superior makes them feel better. Walk away peacefully. The battle they are fighting is not with you; it is with themselves. Protect your spirit from contamination. Stay determined. Your job is to serve God until He leads you to a plan. God will speak to you through scriptures. A wise person knows where their strength comes from during times of trouble, God! Seven things God hates: false witness who lies, haughty eyes, a lying tongue, a heart that devises wicked schemes, hands that shed innocent blood, a person who stirs up conflict, and feet that rush too evil (Proverbs 6:16–19). "Holy Spirit, You are welcome here." Satan cannot read your thoughts, but he can hear your words. Praise God out loud with a loud voice!

I declare: "I search for God and always do His will, rejecting compromise with evil and walking only in His paths."

DECEMBER 20

Let God renew your mind and regenerate your abilities.

For the Word of God is living and powerful, and sharper
than any two-edged sword, piercing even to the center of our
soul and spirit, joints, and marrow, and it is a discerner of
our thoughts and intents of our heart.
Hebrews 4:12 (NKJV; paraphrased)

The Holy Spirit not only empowers but regenerates your whole being. The Word of God has changed my entire life. I live in wholeness. Yield your all to the power of the Holy Spirit. He will clean all areas of your life. It does not serve us to leave home without the Holy Spirit. Take no counsel from anyone who does not seek their instructions from the Holy Spirit. And do not be conformed to this world, be transformed by the renewing of your mind (Romans 12:2). Change requires unpacking and heavy lifting. We can be internally immature, growing older on the outside but staying like a child on the inside. This will sabotage the plan of God because of your internal conflicts with your outside growth. The Word of God will bring you up to speed on the inside, deepening spiritual maturity. "When I was a child, I spoke as a child [...]; but when I became a man, I put away childish things" (1 Corinthians 13:11, NKJV).

I declare: "I pray for a spiritual plan and yield to the Holy Spirit."

DECEMBER 21

How beautiful is it to find someone who asks for nothing more than your company? Guarded by angels. Rely on His promises. Wait for His answers. Believe in His miracles. Rejoice in His goodness. Relax in His presence. Eventually, God will put a person in your pathway who is tired of games. And their loyalty will complete yours. Temporary people give permanent life lessons. Be with someone who wants to love God with you. Faith does not exempt us from difficulties. If you do not get in your Bible, your enemy will get in your business. The more you trust God, the more He amazes you. Effort is between you and you. Your wisdom is from healed pain. Everyone is not your assignment. That is why you are drained. The more you talk, the more you cannot hear God's voice. It is not a secret. Pray, then plan. I was raised to treat the janitor with the same respect as the CEO. "Be still and know that I am God" (Psalm 46:10a, NKJV). Remember, when you forgive, you heal. And by letting go, you grow.

I declare: "Without faith, it is impossible to please and be satisfactory to God. For whoever would come near to God must (necessarily) believe that God exists and that He is the rewarder of those who earnestly and diligently seek Him."

DECEMBER 22

Your greatest contribution may not be something you do but someone you raise. When you feel lost, remember who you are doing it for. I can. I will. When we pray for each other, something supernatural takes place. Take this moment right now and pray for the person who has been on your heart. Love! Rule #1: Never make God. #2: I am sorry; did I roll my eyes out loud? No pain, no gain, zipper up, and pray. Not my strength but His (Zechariah 4:6). It is better to believe you are part of God's plan. Yes, you! Wear clothes that show off your heart and not your body. One day, you will wake up and be glad that you chose to wait on God's plan. Marry someone who makes you fall in love with God every single day. Love is patient, do not rush what you want to last forever. Talk with God; no breath is ever lost. Pray, work, and have faith. My husband is proof that God answers prayers. Ladies, look for the man who respects you, makes you feel safe, and demonstrates faith in God. A relationship with Jesus is attractive: Humbleness, confidence, high standards, faithfulness, and purity. You are the woman some guy is praying for. Love is praying for each other even before you meet. A God-ordered relationship is never rushed. A godly man pursues his girl after he has her heart.

I declare: "I will put You first, Lord, and accept Your will."

DECEMBER 23

May your life preach more loudly than your lips. A fresh start is not a new place; it is a new mindset! Work on becoming the person you would like to meet. Become that person you knew you always could be. Put away complaining; it is a weakness. Self-control only. Not others. Empower yourself and others. Train your brain to do more. Remove "I cannot" from your vocabulary. Think like the person you want to become. Inspiring people to become more is a thousand times more rewarding than thinking of yourself. The way I deal with others reflects the way I want them to deal with me. Me versus me. You always become what you believe; start reading the Word. You can talk your brain into happiness. Try it. Do not be afraid. Just believe (Mark 5:36). When my heart is overwhelmed, lead me to the rock that is higher than me (Psalm 61:2).

I declare: "The word of God that I speak from my mouth will not return to Him empty but will accomplish what He desires and achieve the purpose for which He sent it to me."

DECEMBER 24

"For to us a child is born..." (Luke 6:9a, NIV). Stay close to things that make you feel alive. Stay kind; it is like loaning your strength for that moment instead of reminding them of their weakness. The sounds of baggage wheeling around, seeing that moving sidewalk, and your boarding pass being torn are all comfortable reminders that you are almost home or visiting someone exciting. Every time you see humor in an uncomfortable situation, you and the other person win. That is what I crave. The less you respond to negativity, you will see you will have more peace. When you have done everything you can do, that is when God will step in and do what you cannot do (2 Corinthians 12:10). Kind words are like honey. The side effects of focus for you are less drama, accomplishments, and abundance. The life you were purposed for. You have been anointed by God to break those bad cycles. Generational curses stop with you and me. When you focus on God, the view gets better. If you want to improve your life, immediately unclutter your closet. Often what we hold onto holds us back. Clutter is the enemy of clarity.

I declare: "But thanks be to God, who in Christ always leads us in triumph and through us spreads and makes evident the fragrance of the knowledge of God everywhere."

DECEMBER 25

Can somebody help me brag about God? He is awesome.

He is a healer. The battle belongs to the Lord. I am going to see the victory. The shape of true love is not a diamond. It is a cross. God has made you an answer, never a problem. Stop overthinking and trust. When you enter His presence with praise, He enters your circumstances with power. Sometimes, your faith will make you look stupid until it starts to rain; ask Noah. Worship is not only when you hear the music and organ at church but also choosing to talk to God all day long! God does not make normal; He only makes unique. We get stuck in certain habits because whatever we think about the most grows. One life. Just one. Be that person you want to have in your life. Yesterday is heavy; put it down. We are not victims of our biology; we control our biology by how we think and speak. Life and death are in our own words. Worshiping God protects your brain. Pride is spiritual cancer. When you stay linked to the vine (John 15:5), you get divine inspiration and divine wisdom from God. Stay linked. Praise God even when you do not understand. Praising God for His power and for His Son. Celebrate. That is your power.

I declare: "I am staying linked to God in everything I think, say, and do."

DECEMBER 26

Start where you are and do what you can. Life change depends on you. What is for you will not pass you unless you stop trying. Organize your life. Declare: I am qualified by God. No weapon formed against me shall prosper in Jesus' name (Isaiah 54:17). The hard part about life is getting your mind in shape. Be your own inspiration. Wake up and work on yourself. Your life reflects your mindset style. There is magic in misery. Ask anyone successful where they started and why. Rock bottom is where I started. You may have seen me struggle, but you will never see me quit. Once you get your mind under control, you can conquer that bad habit and that tongue. Work on your weaknesses until they become your strengths. It is never easy, but it will always be worth it. Your well-being is a huge investment. Your life's happiness depends upon the quality of your thoughts. See your worth. If you start right now, before January, your life story will change for the better. You are about to enter a season of consecutive wins.

I declare: "This is my winning season. I dug myself out of depression by claiming the Word of God."

May the tears you cried this year provide nourishment to the soil for your new year.

DECEMBER 27

As we pack up the decorations, give away the rest of the cookies, help our family get back to normal, and get ourselves back to our routine, keep in mind Christmas is truly never over. We carry Him in our hearts all year long. As we plan and press towards our new year, we always make a place for Him in our beautiful new beginnings. Where would we be without Him? Our reunions were fun; the holiday season is a huge setup for everyone. But let's never forget the real reason for the season. How great is our God! We cannot leave home without it. Forget those things behind us and reach forward in all those things that are ahead. My heart will sing how great our God is. Declare: I press toward the goal for the new year prize of the upward call of God in Christ Jesus (Philippians 3:13–14). After all, is this not what we all just celebrated? "We are here just for You, Lord. Set our hearts on You."

I declare: "I press toward the goal for the new year prize of the upward call of God in Christ Jesus."

DECEMBER 28

God created us to be victors, not losers. Do not listen to trash talk, the lies of the devil, no matter who is speaking. Breathe! Lay it all down at His feet. When that situation starts banging on your door, speak the name of Jesus. How many times has God turned that situation around, especially when you started to gear yourself up in fear? Exactly! Now is not the time to stop putting your trust in our *Mighty* God. He has never let you down. The Word is your weapon against the schemes of the enemy. Use your weapons of warfare against that weakness. You know your Father's heart. He can flood your soul right now with His strength, so lift His name on high. He knows you were made for so much more than to merely survive. Joy is unstoppable. Love is unspeakable. Anything is possible with Him. Stop obsessing over and talking about negative problems, or you will make more trouble for yourself. You were made for much more. If God is for you, then who can be against you? The Word, His name, the blood, is your supernatural power. What a beautiful and powerful name it is, Jesus. No name will ever compare. It will pull you out of darkness, breaking all those chains. Stay in that marvelous light. Heaven is for you. He has no rival. His name is above all names!

I declare: "I will call on Jesus in times of trouble."

DECEMBER 29

Do you need special encouragement today? Let cheer be your word. Work on that smile, for it is the best cosmetic, free of charge. Be of good cheer! No one wants to be around miserable. Cheerfulness is unspeakable joy that shows up first on your face (Proverbs 15:13). The God we serve is mighty in battle, and we will not fail. You are going to see His victory, for this battle right here belongs to the Lord. There is a mighty power in the name of Jesus. Do not back down. Declare: I am going to see His victory through my situation. What the enemy meant for evil, He will turn it for good. Worshiping God has your answer. I am walking in victory, and I am walking right over this battle. I am fearless in Jesus. I am a mighty warrior. I am directed by the supernatural power of the Holy Spirit. I will not listen to the defeat of the enemy. I am a prayer warrior. No defeat will I speak. I will not trust in my own abilities. I am holding on to the heart and promises of God. Smile: it is good for your heart, free, and has no excuses. A glad heart makes a cheerful countenance (Proverbs 15:11). Laughter is incredibly healthy no matter what age you are. Be of good cheer (Mark 10:49).

I declare: "I am going to see His victory through my situation. What the enemy meant for evil, He will turn it for good."

DECEMBER 30

File others' opinions right here between "If God is for you" and "then who can be against you!" Your real difficulty is to overcome how you think about yourself. Speak to yourself in the most encouraging way you can. You will never speak to anyone more than yourself. Have standards. Become aware today what you really are worth! You are worth way more than all your failures and your darkness. Do not ever doubt your worth again. Self-love is the key to a lot of your existing situations. Think about all that you are. Write it down and review it. You will do great things. What do you want to accomplish? Eyes forward. Mind focused. Heart prepared. Believe in yourself more. With God, all things are possible (Matthew 19:26). The peace I have now is worth all my past failures. Say goodbye to drama, toxic people, and self-criticism.

Nothing great comes easy. Persistence will make a great you. This is the beginning of the "new" you.

I declare: "I am growing and becoming strong in spirit, filled with wisdom, and the grace (favor and spiritual blessing) of God is upon me."

DECEMBER 31

You have failed! And you will fail again, but that does not mean you are a failure. When you stay stuck in the flesh, you will do fleshy things. To have that power-filled life, you must keep your mind on thoughts that are in line with the Word of God! This will keep your mind set on your power goals. Set your mind on the things above. We all fall. Your thoughts will mold what you think about. If God is for you, then who can be against you (Romans 8:31)? When God holds your hand, He never lets you go (Isaiah 41:13). God will take you places you have never dreamed of. You know what you must do; you just must make seeking God a priority. Do you pray for others as much as you complain about them? If you are not being patient, you have lost half of the battle already. Never stop learning because life will never stop teaching. No time for gossip, distractions, or complaining. It must go. It took letting go to realize I was holding on to nothing. Time heals nothing unless you move along with it. There is a future version of you, so do not quit now. Stay strong. Trust. To the girl I was back then, "I forgive you." Always forgive and sleep with a clean heart. Happiness is, of course, an inside job.

I declare: "God, breathe on me while I sleep tonight that I may wake up healed, whole, empowered, and blessed."

Prayer for Salvation

If you need Jesus and want a personal relationship with Him, pray this simple prayer out loud...

Father God, I love You.

I believe in my heart and confess with my mouth that You,

the Lord Jesus, died on the cross and rose again. Forgive me

of my sins, wash me clean, come into my heart, and heal me.

I am sorry for shutting You out. I want You in my life.

I surrender. I yield. I receive Jesus as my Lord and Savior.

Take me just the way I am.

Now make me everything You want me to be.

I believe I am saved. I am on my way to heaven.

Amen.

Declare these scriptures out loud daily to help guard our mouths.

So shall My word be that goes forth out of My mouth;
It shall not return to Me void,
But it shall accomplish what I please,
And it shall prosper in the thing for which I sent it.

Isaiah 55:11 (NKJV)

Keep your tongue from evil,
And your lips from speaking deceit.

Psalm 34:13 (NKJV)

Right and just lips are the delight of a king, and he loves him
who speaks what is right.

Proverbs 16:13 (AMPC)

Understand [this], my beloved brethren. Let every man be
quick to hear [a ready listener], slow to speak, slow to take
offense and to get angry.

James 1:19 (AMPC)

And whatever you do in word or deed, do all in the name
of the Lord Jesus, giving thanks to God the Father through
Him.

Colossians 3:17 (NKJV)

Do all things without grumbling and faultfinding and
complaining [against God] and questioning and doubting
[among yourselves].

Philippians 2:14 (AMPC)

Declare these scriptures out loud daily to help guard your mouths.

It is not what goes into the mouth of a man that makes him unclean and defiled, but what comes out of the mouth; this makes a man unclean and defiles [him].

Matthew 15:11 (AMPC)

Death and life are in the power of the tongue, and they who indulge in it shall eat the fruit of it [for death or life].

Proverbs 18:21 (AMPC)

Let your speech at all times be gracious (pleasant and win-some), seasoned [as it were] with salt, [so that you may never be at a loss]to know how you ought to answer anyone [who puts a question to you].

Colossians 4:6 (AMPC)

He who guards his mouth keeps his life, but he who opens wide his lips comes to ruin.

Proverbs 13:3 (AMPC)

He who guards his mouth and his tongue keeps himself from troubles.

Proverbs 21:23 (AMPC)

Whoever would love life and see good days must keep their tongue from evil and their lips from deceitful speech.

1 Peter 3:10 (NIV)

I give God all the glory from the bottom of my heart. There are no simple solutions to life's problems. It is a fight of faith that gives you hope and trust in the only One who holds your future in His hands. We are in this life together! Iron sharpens iron.

About the Author

Susan (Suzi) Julian Yelvington was born and raised in Utica, New York, and resides in Florida with her husband, Gary. She has worked in the corporate arena for over forty years, mentoring, encouraging, and building powerful relationships through her gentle spirit. Suzi gives back to her community by mentoring and speaking engagements. She feels particularly drawn to organizations intended to support individuals through the

Christian faith. Her public presentations over the past few years have targeted women and youth populations. Suzi is the author of multiple devotional books.

Printed in the USA
CPSIA information can be obtained
at www.ICGtesting.com
LVHW020820210724
786028LV00010B/195